◆ HOW TO CLIMB SERIES ◆

Better Bouldering

John Sherman

FALCON®

CHOCKSTONE®

1 2 3 4 5 6 7 8 9 10 MG 05 04 03 02 01 00

COVER PHOTO: Split Boulder, Fringe of Death Canyon, Photo by Stewart M. Green

All interior photos by author unless otherwise noted

ISBN 1-57540-087-1

PUBLISHED AND DISTRIBUTED BY
Falcon Purblishing, Inc.
P.O. Box 1718
Helena, MT 59624

OTHER BOOKS IN THIS SERIES:
How to Rock Climb!
Advanced Rock Climbing
Climbing Anchors
More Climbing Anchors
Sport Climbing
Big Walls
Flash Training!
I Hate to Train Performance Guide for Climbers
Knots for Climbers
Nutrition for Climbers
Building Your Own Indoor Climbing Wall
Gym Climb
Clip and Go!
Self-Rescue
Top Roping
How to Climb 5.12!

Preface

At first the idea of writing a how-to book on bouldering seemed ridiculous. I can tell you how to boulder in one sentence: find some boulders and climb them. Nevertheless, going bouldering is one thing, bouldering well and enjoying it quite another. The time-honored path to bouldering success depends on learning from one's mistakes. The more mistakes you make, the more you learn. A better way is to learn from my mistakes—this book is bursting with 22 years' worth.

Many of bouldering's tricks and strategies aren't common knowledge, and some have never reached print. My publisher convinced me there would be merit, if not money, to be had by putting this information in print. As well, somewhere along the line a mote of maturity entered my body (musta sneaked in with the fat cells and gray hairs), and I no longer feel the need to keep these tricks secret.

When I first started bouldering, there were no books on the subject. There was, however, a terrific community of boulderers at Indian Rock who befriended and taught me despite my bumbling. Though I learned much of what's in this book after those formative years, it was the Indian Rock crew that taught me the most important lesson: above all, bouldering should be fun.

I thank the following people for their comments on the manuscript: Jeff Achey, Jim Belcer, Scott Blunk, Chris Dunn, Chris Jones, and Neal Kaptain. I also thank all the people who appear in the photos. Thanks too to John Gill and Jim Holloway for use of their photos.

This book is dedicated to Craig and Mig (who first took me bouldering), and to the Indian Rock crew: Harrison, Nat, Scott, Fred, Steve, Bert, Bird, Amy, Dave, Rob, Mike, Becca, Kalen, Russ, Bruce, Jim, Sherry, Eben, Duncan, Hombre, and the others whose names and faces got mixed up in the blender of my memory.

WARNING: CLIMBING IS A SPORT WHERE YOU MAY BE SERIOUSLY INJURED OR DIE

READ THIS BEFORE YOU USE THIS BOOK.

This is an instruction book to rock climbing, a sport which is inherently dangerous. You should not depend solely on information gleaned from this book for your personal safety. Your climbing safety depends on your own judgment based on competent instruction, experience, and a realistic assessment of your climbing ability.

There is no substitute for personal instruction in rock climbing and climbing instruction is widely available. You should engage an instructor or guide to learn climbing safety techniques. If you misinterpret a concept expressed in this book, you may be killed or seriously injured as a result of the misunderstanding. Therefore, the information provided in this book should be used only to supplement competent personal instruction from a climbing instructor or guide. Even after you are proficient in climbing safely, occasional use of a climbing instructor is a safe way to raise your climbing standard and learn advanced techniques.

There are no warranties, either expressed or implied, that this instruction book contains accurate and reliable information. There are no warranties as to fitness for a particular purpose or that this book is merchantable. Your use of this book indicates your assumption of the risk of death or serious injury as a result of climbing's risks and is an acknowledgement of your own sole responsibility for your climbing safety.

C O N T E N T S

INTRODUCTION 1

1: GEAR 5

2: SAFETY 13

3: THE ART OF DYNAMIC MOVEMENT 27

4: FINESSE AND POWER 37

5: MORE BOULDERING TRICKS 45

6: THE MENTAL GAME 59

7: STRATEGY AND AVOIDING MISTAKES 65

8: HEALTH AND INJURIES 71

9: FIRST ASCENTS 77

10: MORE BOULDERING GAMES 85

11: TRAINING 89

12: PATHS TO SUCCESS 91

APPENDIX 95

INDEX 98

BETTER BOULDERING

JOHN SHERMAN

Pulling down in the Black Hole at Morrison, Colorado.

Introduction

In 1975 I was a pudgy high school junior who couldn't do a single pull-up. Outside of knocking down a few beers with my buddies, I had few interests I can remember, and no passions. Then one day a couple of drinking buddies took me bouldering at Indian Rock, in Berkeley. I was pathetic, a regular Bob Euker of bouldering. It took me multiple days just to scale Beginner's Crack, a route most tyros do on their first outing. Nevertheless, I persevered. A few visits later I pulled off a tricky move around an arête that was thwarting much better climbers. For the first time ever, I felt I possessed some athletic aptitude. I was hooked. I bought a pair of EBs and went to the rock nearly every day after school until I graduated. By that time I was cranking 16 chin-ups off the door jamb in the English classroom, and my wannabe beer belly disappeared. Bouldering became the defining passion in my life. Where I chose to live, the friends I made, the jobs I took, the lack of sex—all were influenced by my need to boulder. Bouldering changed my life forever: it gave me focus, healthy exercise, an outlet for stress, a positive self-attitude, and some cool scars. It can give you all of these as well.

Bouldering is a difficult and sometimes frustrating pastime. I know. I nearly quit after making it up only one problem on my first day (this one even easier than Beginner's Crack). The success on that one problem, as well as the fear and exhilaration, kept me going. As did each subsequent success. I realize now that the problems I couldn't climb drove me as well. Somewhere a marvelous transition took place: I was no longer "at war" with the rock; I was "at one" with it. The boulders became my friends, not my adversaries. Hopefully, the tips in this book will improve your bouldering and help you to become "at one" with the rock.

This book is not written to tell you how to boulder, but rather how to boulder better. A beginning level of climbing knowledge is assumed on the part of the reader. If you desire a primer on basic climbing movement techniques, I suggest reading *How to Rock Climb!* by John Long in this same series.

I'm sure we'd all like to be the Michael Jordan of bouldering. Realistically, few, if any of us, possess that kind of athletic ability. I'm of only average athletic ability. Fortunately, so too was Larry Bird—and it never stopped him. At one point I did get strong. When I was 20, I could do 50 pull-ups, but I was lousy at utilizing that strength. Ten years later, I could do less than half as many pull-ups, but I was doing problems I wouldn't have dreamed possible when I was 20, because I was using my brain as well as my arms.

Being smart will get you up more boulders than being strong. This book aims to make you smarter. We'll focus on techniques specific to bouldering, such as spotting; and those best expressed on the boulders, like dynamic moves. We'll also discuss some of the most common movement mistakes and how to cure them. In addition, we will delve into the nature of the sport, the gear used, and bouldering ratings. Lastly, we'll explore a number of ways top boulderers have approached the sport, and how you can use these approaches to improve your own bouldering.

This book can be viewed as merely a compendium of how-to tips and tricks, or it can be an invitation to explore the philosophical aspects of the sport. In line with the latter approach, the text features numerous sidebars containing various "hero stories" taken from my personal experiences. They're there to further illustrate points made in the text, as well as demonstrate the growth of a boulderer. If you would rather not bathe in the glow/stench (circle one or both) of my ego, you can safely skip these asides and rest assured that you are not missing out on vital technical information.

NOTE: The photos in this book span a three-decade time period. At the time of writing, there is no legal access to the following pictured problems and areas: *Splatter High* and *The Devil in Chris Jones* at Hueco Tanks; the Wilford problem pictured on p. 23; *Howard's Knob, The Juggernaut, The Ripper Traverse,* UC Berkeley buildering and the Hagermeister Boulders. In the future, access might be lost to more of the problems pictured. Problems pictured in this book are included for instructional purposes only. The author and the publisher do not condone climbing on problems without legal access.

THE BOULDERING GAME

Bouldering has the reputation of being the simplest of all climbing games: you don't need an expensive rack or rope, you don't need a lot of time—you don't even need a partner. All you need is boulders and desire.

In its broadest sense, bouldering is defined as unroped rock climbing close enough to the ground that a fall would not be fatal. Most people would add that bouldering should be highly gymnastic and relatively low risk.

At its simplest, bouldering can be nothing more than playing on rocks. Carried to extreme levels, it can be an intense battle against oneself and nature. Because you can try dozens of different climbs each time you go out bouldering, you can steer each session to match your mood. You can pack in more hard moves in a day than with any other kind of climbing. On the other hand, you needn't always throw yourself at the hardest problem around. The following very incomplete list hints at the variety the bouldering experience can provide: climbing a problem with the most holds; climbing a problem with the least holds; off-routing selected holds to add difficulty; trying the lowest possible start; playing follow-the-leader; trying to do a problem fastest; doing laps on a problem; searching out first ascents; repeating a problem in fewer tries than it has been done before; wiring a problem until it is effortless;

doing the longest problem, the shortest problem, the prettiest problem, or the most strenuous problem; seeing how many times you can do a given problem in a single session; trying to do the most problems you can in a session; seeing who can do the longest jump between boulder tops; climbing blindfolded…and so forth. You might approach bouldering as training for roped climbs or you might sell your harness and devote your life to the small stones.

Ninety percent of the time bouldering is practiced above a good landing; no higher than the boulderer is willing to jump from. Risk is minimal, hence the boulderer can concentrate on the moves and not the danger. On occasion, the boulderer will try problems over bad landings, but with the assurance of a good spotter and/or padding over the rocks below.

High bouldering, in which a fall is long enough to cause injury, has provided me with some of the most intense experiences in my climbing career. But as the rewards are so great, so is the risk. Jumping off is not an option. When asked where I draw the line between high bouldering and soloing, I say, "If you fall high bouldering you will get hurt. If you fall soloing, you will die." Obviously this is a perilous game and only recommended for expert boulderers with outstanding judgment. For most climbers it is a small or negligible part of their bouldering experience. Nevertheless, because the techniques and tricks of the high boulderer are worth learning for every boulderer, a fair portion of this book is devoted to them.

I hope this book will raise your bouldering standards by inspiring you to always bring yourself up to the level of a problem and never bring a problem down to your level. View each new problem as a challenge set forth for you by nature. Adapt yourself to meet that challenge. I can guarantee that this approach yields the most bouldering satisfaction and the best path toward mastery. As well, it's a good way to approach life in general.

Two ends of the spectrum: Dave Altman (top) uses a sit-down start to make the most out of a problem on the "Ape's Traverse" Boulder at Indian Rock, Berkeley, California, while the author takes it high off the deck on the East Side of the Sierras, California.

"I hope I didn't forget anything." Bouldering requires a minimal amount of gear, but as in all modern sports, there are tech weenies. The author pondering his gear selection during a multi-month road trip.

Gear

The only gear really needed to go bouldering is boulders. But since we live in a high-tech age of electric can-openers and space shuttles, it's only natural that specialized gear exists to help us scale boulders.

THE FOUR ESSENTIALS

At the bare minimum, a modern boulderer should carry the four essentials: rock shoes, a bag of gymnastics chalk (though some purists eschew this aid), a toothbrush to clean chalk and dirt from holds, and a carpet patch on which to wipe one's shoes.

Shoes

This is a very personal matter. On bouldering trips I've carried up to six different pairs of shoes to be prepared for any problem: stiff edging boots; loose, comfy, warm-up boots; heel-hooking shoes; slippers for thin cracks and pockets; high tops for bad landings; and an all-around shoe.

If you aren't fortunate enough to have a boot sponsor and can only afford one pair of shoes, I would suggest getting an all-around shoe with a high top to provide ankle support when you jump or fall onto uneven ground. As well, a shoe with ample rands is a plus for heel hooking and instep smears. Don't get stuck on the brand your hero wears: his or her foot may not be shaped like yours. Furthermore, don't buy the "Our rubber is stickier" claims. As of 1997, different rubbers are so similar as to be indistinguishable in blind tests. Ignore the ads and believe your feet. Buy the brand that fits your foot best and is most durable. The climbers in the ads get their shoes for free, so they don't care how durable they are. A resoler who's been in business for years and has resoled hundreds of pairs of shoes is a good person to ask which brands are most durable.

You will be jumping from boulders frequently. Shoes that pinch your toes may edge a bit better, but will hurt like hell whenever you hit the ground.

Chalk And Chalk Bag

Climbers use gymnastics chalk to keep hands and fingers dry and to reduce the greasy feel on handholds. It is composed of magnesium carbonate and comes in blocks, powder, or a combination lumpy powder. Which form you choose is a matter of personal preference; they all work well. Powder, however, is more prone to blowing out of chalk bags on windy days and to spillage if a chalk bag tips over. Some companies distribute "chalk socks" that are porous fabric sacks filled with powdered chalk and kept in one's chalk bag. (These are

The four essentials

commonly called "chalkballs," though one company has trademarked that name.) These help prevent spillage and keep chalk dust to a minimum, the latter being an important consideration in climbing gyms or for climbers with breathing problems such as bronchitis or asthma. Many of these chalk-balls are refillable. You can make your own from an old sock.

Lately some manufacturers have added "secret drying ingredients" to their chalk. Some climbers find this improves performance; others can't tell the difference. If you already have dry skin, these "super chalks" may cause excessive drying and subsequent skin splitting. (See Chapter 8 for tips on keeping skin healthy.)

Because the majority of chalk bags are basically the same, most people choose their chalk bags on the basis of how cool they look. Some people, especially those with big hands, like big bags they can sink their entire mitt into. Others prefer the light weight of a bag that accepts only fingertips. The only really essential feature to look for on a bouldering chalk bag is a slot, pocket, or loop to hold your toothbrush. On most hard boulder problems you will not be able to let go and chalk up. Therefore, I suggest finding a bag that will sit on the ground and not tip over and spill. Years ago, most bags featured collapsible mid-sections that helped prevent spills—a good idea that fell victim to fashion trends. A few manufacturers make chalk pots—big, pear-shaped chalk bags designed to sit on the ground.

You wear two shoes, so why not wear two chalk bags? On longer problems where I have to chalk up in the midst of the climb, I like to wear a chalk bag on each hip. I look about as suave as Barney the Dinosaur, but this system works great. I always know where to dip, and the energy I save not fishing around for my chalk bag while hanging from one hand more than makes up for the extra weight.

Toothbrush

Your old retired brush with the black algae growing up the bristles will do, but given that this is the least expensive piece of bouldering gear, why not splurge and buy a new toothbrush with a full head of firm bristles? If you're too cheap for that, go pinch granny's denture brush. These sport very firm bristles and some come with a chisel-shaped front row that easily cleans narrow crevices.

To clean holds beyond your reach, make an extendobrush (or bubbabrush in the boulderer's vernacular). This can be as simple as taping a toothbrush to a stick, or you can go all the way with a telescoping handle and attached blow tube. My personal bubbabrush consists of an old golf club shaft (buy the longest club you find in the barrel at the thrift shop) with a denture brush held on the end with small pipe clamps. A plastic blow tube enters the butt/handle end of the shaft. Because the shaft gradually narrows toward the brush end, the force of the air rushing through the tube is concentrated and does a great job of blowing loose chalk, dirt, and debris off of holds.

Carpet Patch

A carpet patch is used to wipe the soles of your boots on immediately before getting on a problem. You can either cut a square from an old carpet, or go to a carpet store and ask if they have any sample patches of discontinued lines they'd give you (or sell to you for a buck or two). The carpet store samples have finished edges so they won't unravel on you. Never leave your rug fixed at the boulders. They become dirty so quickly (and muddy if it rains) that they become useless. Furthermore, they are trash, plain and simple, and give a homeless hideout look to any boulderfield. By always keeping your personal rug with you, you can keep it clean. It thereby cleans your boots better, increasing your chance of succeeding on a given problem.

OTHER DESIRABLE GEAR

Sketchpad

Sketchpads are foam-cushioned mats used to take the sting out of bouldering falls. They are also called crash pads or crash mats (the original name referred to the device you wanted when things got sketchy). Used intelligently, sketchpads allow one to push harder on the boulders. Until a few years ago, all sketchpads were homemade numbers consisting of foam sandwiched between two layers of carpet. Today, several manufacturers offer slicker models.

Many climbers view sketchpads as devices merely to protect against bruised feet. They have trouble justifying a $100-plus investment in a glorified chunk of foam. But sketchpads have a far greater benefit than minimizing stone bruise. Imagine jumping off your kitchen table and onto the linoleum floor 15 times a day, 3 days a week, for 10 years straight. Now imagine how bad your back, your hips, your knees, and your feet would feel after those ten years. Yep, you'd feel like a king—Rodney King. The cumulative effect of bouldering falls can be crippling. Moreover, bouldering falls commonly create acute injuries such as bruised heels and broken feet. There's no sense in becoming an Advil poster child—investing in a good sketchpad is an investment in your long-term health.

The most important component of any sketchpad is the foam. Too soft and you'll feel like you just received a Singapore foot caning. Too stiff and your skeleton will take the shock before the foam does its job. Your weight and bouldering style should determine which pad you buy. Having fallen on more sketchpads more times than probably anyone else, I've come up with the following rule of thumb for checking foam quality and consistency. Stand on the sketchpad with both feet. If your weight fully compresses the pad without jumping up and down, the pad is too soft. If you stand with all your weight on one foot, it should compress nearly all the way down—a one-inch hop should compress it fully. Obviously, Mary Lou Retton would pick a softer pad than Hulk Hogan. If you only take very short falls, you can get away with a softer pad than if you frequently take very long falls.

Mark Wilford on "Right Eliminator," Horsetooth Reservoir.

Some pads allow you to add or subtract foam to adapt to your needs. Some also have two densities of foam: a thick chunk of open cell and a thin slice of closed cell. There are two theories on using these. One says to lay the closed cell on the bottom as the final protection against stone bruise if you fully compress the open cell above. The other says put the closed cell on top to distribute the force of a fall out over more of the open cell foam below. Pads are made both ways, but in practice you can just flip them for the desired effect—closed cell down for a softer landing on short falls, closed cell up for a stiffer landing on long bombs or if your open cell foam has gone mushy.

Quality sketchpads are not cheap. Good, durable foam costs about as much per pound as filet mignon. It will last for years before wearing out. Cheap foam costs about as much per pound as hamburger. A pad made of cheap foam may work well for the first month or two, but will quickly deteriorate and soften.

Imagine swapping a Kevlar vest for cashmere. Then imagine a bullet coming at you.

The best size of sketchpad to get is the biggest one you're willing to carry. The longer the approach to your favorite area, the smaller a pad you might want to own. Also, the higher off the ground you boulder, the greater you risk missing a small pad when you fall. While climbing the notorious Gill route on the Thimble, I remember my 3-foot wide sketchpad looking like a napkin.

The original homemade sketchpads had carpet exteriors that were heavy but durable. The foam wore out before the carpet. Store-bought models save weight by having pack cloth exteriors. I have seen some of these wear out prematurely. Check for heavy-weight pack cloth and for double-stitched seams. Most models also have some sort of fleece covering on one side to wipe your feet on. This is no substitute for carrying your own carpet patch, as the sketchpad is often not positioned at the base of the problem. Therefore, you need a carpet patch at the base anyway. Notwithstanding, this fleece cover makes for comfy lounging between attempts. It also provides extra friction for upside-down placements on steep slabs. (More on placing sketchpads in Chapter 2.)

Most sketchpads fold for easy carrying. Straps or Velcro flaps keep it folded. Check how convenient the straps are to use—some are a pain in the hindquarters. Also, can you stash shoes and chalk bag inside without them falling out?

Any number of bells and whistles can be attached to your sketchpad: the most useful being shoulder straps for backpack-style carrying, and a leash for dragging it under a moving climber. Multiple attachment points for the leash can be handy for oddball anchoring situations.

Skin Kit

A honking flapper the size of a nickel need not end your session if you have a skin kit along. A skin kit contains a roll of breathable athletic tape, nail clippers, an emery board or patch, a tube of Krazy Glue, and a can of TufSkin or bottle of tincture of benzoin. Band-Aids and antibacterial ointment (such as Neosporin) are needed for post-session treatments. (See Chapter 8 for use of the skin kit.)

Knee Pads

Knee bars are often the key to success on many problems. Big soccer-style knee pads are clumsy and have a tendency to rotate when smeared against the rock. More stable are the thin neoprene pads that look like a small section of a wet suit.

Helmet

Despite allegations that my skull is thicker than the former Berlin Wall, I have suffered multiple concussions from occasionally landing on my head instead of my feet. I have worn a helmet many times when bouldering without a spot. Go

*Bruce Pottenger in the
Buttermilks, California.*

ahead and say it: dorkus amongus. I feel that a bicycle helmet is a better choice for bouldering than a climbing helmet. Bouldering falls are very much like falls off a bicycle, and bike helmets are designed to withstand blows both to the sides and top of your head. Climbing helmets, on the other hand, are designed to stop falling rocks from caving in the top of your skull. Most climbing helmets provide little side impact protection, though some of the newer models are trending in this direction.

Ego-swelling Combat Tale #1

One of the most satisfying first ascents I've done is called Best of the Best. The 40-minute approach, the longest in Hueco Tanks, put off most potential spotters, so several times I went up there alone. This 25-foot roof ran above a stepped slab landing with potential for serious injury if one landed on the edge of a step. To protect myself I positioned a sketch pad over the most hazardous step. Then I stuffed a folded ensolite pad down the back of a pair of baggy shorts and inside my T-shirt to protect my spine. Furthermore, I wore a bicycle helmet. A couple of kneepads and I could have been taking snaps in the NFL. These precautions allowed me to try moves I wouldn't other-wise have tried without a spotter. Despite looking like a rodeo clown, I eventually succeeded. As I sat atop the boulder, all that protective gear strapped to me could not stop the good feelings from soaking in.

MISCELLANEOUS GEAR

In some areas, such as the southeastern US, vegetation grows quickly. In such areas, pruning shears can keep problems open, but if not used with a measure of respect for the local ecology, they can get entire areas closed. I've put up thousands of first ascents and have never found a chain saw to be necessary.

To clean wet holds, a towel or T-shirt comes in handy (more on using these later), though I've heard one climber claim a box of maxi-pads works best. Sometimes this may not be enough. One of the wackiest tools I've carried is a small propane torch lashed to an extension pole. I needed a bouldering fix badly and the rocks were dripping. A few minutes with the torch and I was good to go and the DTs went away. Still, I wouldn't recommend habitually climbing with a torch because of the expense and the potential, if you overheat holds, that they may weaken or flake off due to expansion and contraction. Such exfoliation can be serious. The Robbins Problem on Yosemite's famed Columbia Boulder peeled off due to campfires built under it. Furthermore, the time involved torching holds usually limits you to one or two problems per session. Watching TV or working on one's wet hold technique are probably better options.

Joey Henson spots Jimmy "The Griz"
Horton as he struggles over the lip
on "Raw Terror," Blowing Rock,
North Carolina.

**Safety**

CHAPTER 2

In case you go bouldering before you finish reading this book, let's get to the most important information right now. Safety should be a prime concern of all boulderers. Much of what is written in this chapter is here to prepare you for the worst-case scenario of a long fall onto a bad landing. Some of this might make bouldering sound overly scary and serious. However, the chances of a bouldering session ending in a closed casket funeral are virtually nil. Nevertheless, twisted ankles and broken bones are common. This chapter will discuss the risks of bouldering and how to minimize them.

FALLING AND JUMPING

In bouldering, virtually every fall is a ground fall. If it isn't, you've probably either ledged-out or fallen into a tree. Naturally, either scenario can be about as fun as a low blow from heavyweight hopeful Andrew Golatta. Fortunately, there are techniques to minimize injury.

Good Landings

I consider a good landing to be flat or only slightly inclined, free of obstructions, and relatively soft (e.g., dirt or sand—not a rock slab or concrete sidewalk).

With a good landing, ideally one will fall feet-first and onto a sketchpad. When you land, suck up the impact with your legs like a skier hitting a mogul. In extreme cases you might bottom out, your legs fully bent, butt-to-heels and knee-to-chin.

If your body hits a good landing at an angle, you will not be able to suck up the impact with the knees. Instead, roll with the fall like a judo master. Be sure the landing is free of obstructions before you get on the problem. You don't need to be rolling over a half-full beer, your ghetto blaster, and into some dog poop.

On less-than-vertical walls, you might hit the wall as you fall. Push off the wall as you fall so you land clear of the base of the rock. On low-angle slabs (60 degrees or less) you can turn around (face away from the rock) and run down the slab as you fall. Be sure you have room to run after you hit the ground.

WARNING: A nice flat landing doesn't guarantee a safe fall. The North Face of the Mushroom Boulder in Hueco Tanks has one of the smoothest, flattest dirt landings around, yet many climbers have broken wrists when they failed to land on their feet. Two climbers even broke both wrists. You find out who your friends are when you can't wipe for yourself. Don't take good landings for granted and maintain a measure of respect for the dangers involved in bouldering. When available, always use a spotter and a sketchpad.

Use your legs to suck up the impact of landing.

Bad Landings

Some sickos, such as myself, believe that a nasty landing adds spice to a problem, heightening the adrenaline buzz and increasing the feeling of accomplishment when one succeeds. Some of the best boulder problems in the world have bad landings. There are two basic ways to approach problems with bad landings: run away or deal with it.

Running away is also known as discretion and is not a bad quality to have. Be honest with yourself as to your abilities. Hurtling head-first toward a stack of broken blocks is a bad time to find out you aren't ready for a given problem. Boulder problems rarely disappear at night, so you can always come back later. For every twisted high-ball problem I've done, I've seen a dozen I wouldn't try because I felt the risk was too great.

Dealing with it involves carefully analyzing the landing and the directions you might fall. The first thing to check is if your head or spine will hit anything. If so, pad that surface, alert your spotter, and/or wear a helmet. Next, check for branches that might skewer you, tree roots you might twist an ankle on, and so forth. Know where these hazards are before you go up on a problem. I have some nice scars on my back from tearing a hold off a traverse and not knowing there was a splintered tree stump right behind me.

Some bad landing problems consist of multi-level landings, neighboring walls, or boulders you might carom off of.

Way Bad Landings

On extremely uneven landings I prefer not to use a sketchpad so I can see exactly where I'll hit. This way I can aim for the top of the one flat, solid stone available, or straddle the tree root if necessary. When landings are this bad, it pays not to fall, but often one may be forced to jump. Before you go up, know where the danger zones and the safety zones are. Be prepared to jump for the safety zones.

When a landing is nothing but jumbled rocks, and no dirt safety zones or single boulders exist large enough to land on, the boulder run comes into play. It consists of falling or jumping off a problem, then running tiptoe across the tops of the rocks at high speed until one reaches safety or can stop oneself. Imagine Fred Astaire tossed into a mosh pit and dancing across the tops of everyone's heads to get away—that's the boulder run. Generally, this technique is risky: one false step and you could break a leg. Hence, this is a desperation tactic done only when one lands in such a place. It helps to have some kind of sideways momentum when one hits the landing, either from kicking off the rock face just before one reaches the landing, or by pushing off immediately from the first rock one hits. A spotter will only get in the way if you have to do a boulder run. If you think this is your best chance to survive a fall, then I recommend forgoing the sketchpad and the spotter and be prepared to dance.

Clearing Bad Landings

One way to cope with bad landings is to clear them of obstructions and turn them into good landings. This job is commonly left up to the first ascensionist. If he or she chose to clear away more or less than you would, then that was his or her decision and you should respect it. If you don't like the landing on an established boulder problem, go to a different problem that suits your tastes. Other than removing cheater stones (whoever left them there should have done this) or recent debris (say a fallen tree limb), it's best to leave landings as you found them. This way everyone can have the same experience as the first ascensionist.

But The Landing Sucks And I Just Gotta Do That Problem...

A given problem may captivate you so much that you feel you must climb it. Unfortunately, the macho jerk who put it up opted not to clear away the rusty ship anchors and barnacle-encrusted stones at the base. Somehow he felt this added to the thrill of the problem. You, however, would prefer not to risk a trip to the hospital. What do you do? You can toss a top-rope on the problem, you can wait until you are good enough to do it unroped over the bad landing, or you can try and clear the landing. The first two options show respect for the first ascensionist and the climbing community. They are your best choices. If the problem really means a lot to you, then it's probably worth waiting for until you can do it cordless. Some folks will justify the third choice, claiming they are doing a public service by making the problem safe. Fostering disrespect amongst the climbing community, however, is not a public service. If you don't respect others' first ascents, don't expect anyone to respect yours.

Predetermining Fall Angles

This is one of the keys to safe bouldering. Previsualizing sequences to a problem is a common technique that helps one psych up and climb efficiently (more about this later). It is also important to previsualize falling off a problem. Imagine as many scenarios as you can: if that left-hand layaway snaps, I'll end up in the bushes to the

A split second after his feet starting sliding, Adam Massey turns outward to run down "Initial Friction" in Yosemite Valley. Had he faced toward the rock and slid down, he would have lost rubber off his shoes and maybe some skin off his hands as well as risking smashing his shins on the lip at the base of the slab.

Left: Jeff Johnson climbing "The Wave" at the Swimming Hole, Southern California. On problems with very bad landings like this, it is best to ditch the sketchpad and take your chances on a boulder run instead.

Fall angle analysis #1

Hillary Harris on "Three Star Arête," Hueco Tanks. If Hillary's right hand pops, she will pivot to the left around her left handhold and hit the ground around point A. Should her left hand pop, she will pivot to the right and land at point B. Should her right foot pop, she'll drop down and right; if her left hand pops off first, she'll continue to the right and land at point B; if her right hand pops first, she'll pivot around her left arm and land at point C. If her left foot pops and her left hand goes before her right, she'll land at point D; if it's the other way around and her right hand goes before her left, she'll land at point E. If both hands or feet pop simultaneously she'll fall straight down to point F. So where would she most likely fall? Knowing that Hillary is strong as a gorilla, I would doubt that her hands would ever pop off this move. However, the left handhold is so incut as to be potentially fragile, and if it breaks she'll land at point B. As well, the left foothold is much smaller than the right and the chance of popping off it is greater; should this happen, she'll land at D or E, but most likely she could hang on to her hand holds and not fall off. If I were spotting her for this move, I would position myself near point B but be ready for anything.

Fall angle analysis #2

Jonny Woodward in Little Cottonwood Canyon, Utah. Should Jonny's hand pop during this move, his feet would catapult him to the right and his body would be falling horizontally with great potential for a head injury. Should his feet pop, he would swing off to the right as well, but in this case his feet would swing toward the ground causing his body to fall vertically—a much safer scenario. Either case is possible on this hard greasy move. The spotter should be positioned to Jonny's right and be prepared to grab him under the armpits should Jonny's hand come off, or grab Jonny's waist should his feet come off.

Fall angle analysis #3

Brad Tomlin on "Bachar Roof," Horsetooth Reservoir, Colorado. This problem is too close to the ground to effectively spot, but fall angle analysis would help with the placement of a sketchpad. Brad is lunging for hold A, if he comes up short on his lunge, he will pivot down and land at point B. As well, if his feet pop, his right arm undercling would thrust his body toward point B. If he sticks the lunge and his feet come off, he will swing outward—if the momentum of this swing pulls his right hand off he will fly far outward and land out of the photo to the left of the frame, unless he can hold on to hold A. If his right hand comes off before he hits the target hold, he will land anywhere along the line from C to D depending how far along in the swing he is when that hand pops. This is a very common roof lunge scenario and would also be valid if this problem were high enough off the deck to be spotted. Because potential falls can occur over such wide real estate, roof lunges are best done with multiple spotters. If only one spotter is available, then one must weigh all the factors—the odds of hitting the target hold, the potential to hang on the target hold should everything else come off, how good the footholds are and so forth—before positioning the spotter.

NOTE: These sample analyses don't take every contingency into consideration. For example, if the space shuttle was to crash into the back of the Three Star Arête Boulder, Hillary would probably land somewhere in Albuquerque. As well, these samples only analyze a single move. Out in the field you'd analyze fall angles for the entire problem, paying extra attention to the hardest and most hazardous moves. The idea behind these samples is to introduce you to the thinking process involved in fall angle analysis. As you look at the other pictures in this book, try to analyze them as well.

The author on "Splatter High" at Hueco Tanks, Texas. If I fall from here, I would carom off the rock under me on my way to the ground. Therefore, my spotter is facing the boulder behind me, ready to catch a fall from that angle. A pre-jump was used to position the spotter.

right; if I can't push the mantel, I might topple over backwards; If my left foot pops off that nubbin, I'll shoot down and to the left, and so on. Experience and/or a degree in physics will help you figure out the angles. Discuss these possibilities with your spotters. Tell them which moves you feel you might fall off of. Then they can already be in position. Previsualizing falls is only a safety precaution. Don't let it psych you out. Do it for every problem and it will become standard operating procedure.

Pre-jumps

The more experience you have, the easier it will be to predetermine fall angles. Sometimes, however, you can't figure out where you'll land by looking at a problem. In this case, I will sometimes climb up to the move in question, give it just enough effort to put my body into the position it will be in when trying the move, then jump off from that position. Because I am forcing the fall, I am prepared to land on my feet and suck up the impact, hopefully with the help of my spotter. This simulated fall, or pre-jump, should give you a very good idea of the trajectory a real, unexpected fall from that point will take. You can then position your spotter and sketchpads accordingly. In certain situations where one might carom off a wall or neighboring boulder before hitting the ground, one may pre-jump, not from the move itself, but from the point you will bounce off the wall or that neighboring boulder (granted you can establish yourself at this point). This will make for a shorter, less dangerous pre-jump.

I have yet to be injured from a pre-jump, but that is because I use it sparingly. If a landing is so bad that the risk of injury during a pre-jump is nearly as great as that from an unrehearsed fall, I will not do a pre-jump.

The Stone Toss

This is a good trick to use with, or instead of, a pre-jump to determine where one might land. It is generally less accurate than a pre-jump, but is virtually free of risk. With the stone toss, I toss a stone, stick, or other object up the boulder to the point where I think I might fall off. I watch its trajectory after it bounces off the boulder and where it lands (hopefully in the middle of a sketchpad). I repeat this several times. The best results come when the stone bounces a short way out from the wall before landing, instead of ricocheting straight down. This is because climbers usually pop away from the rock when they fall, then drop. This technique works best for straight-down falls, and is of limited use for falls with a component of sideways trajectory.

Spotting is the technique used to break a boulderer's fall and steer him or her to a safe landing. Spotting is a technique that takes time to master. As a spotter, your partners count on you for their safety. Spotting is not a chore, it is a sacred trust.

Let me pound the point in a bit harder. A good attitude is the most important characteristic of a good spotter. Many of the greatest ascents in the history of bouldering were done only because the boulderer had a trustworthy spotter who took pride in his assignment. The "I'll spot you on your project, if you'll spot me on mine" attitude is sure to generate listless, ineffective spots.

The ideal spotter would have the reflexes of Bruce Lee, the lateral movement and quickness of Martina Navritilova, and the strength and size of Shaquille O'Neal. Of course no such person exists, but Scott Blunk comes close at 6'7", 220 pounds, and a master of martial arts. Still, those qualifications would be all for naught if it weren't for Scott's superior attitude and technique. These anyone can develop, even if you're built like Pauly Shore or Michael Jackson. A superior attitude comes from taking pride in one's duty and striving to always better your technique.

Ego-swelling Combat Tale #2

I was bouldering on Scott Blunk's ranch in Wyoming several years back, trying to bag the second ascent of a wild diagonal lunge problem he had put up. I would fly for the lip, come up short, then arc over to the left where Scott would break my fall. This happened many times as I continued to work on the problem. On my last try, I was all coiled up, ready to blast for the lip. Suddenly, the finger rail I was yarding on snapped. I launched backward and headfirst like a backstroker starting a race. My noggin was on trajectory to land in a patch of stones and cactus several yards right of where I had been landing. There was no warning, unlike the previous falls, but because he focused his entire attention on spotting me, not just watching me, Scott made a save that would have highlighted ESPN's "Plays Of The Week." I didn't even nick the ground.

Spotting Priorities

When spotting, you are not required to catch the falling climber like a football or a ballerina. The spotter's number one priority is to protect the boulderer's head and spine.

The spotter's priorities, in order:

1. *Protect the boulderer's head and spine.* If the spotter fails to protect the boulderer's head and/or spine and an injury results, then the spotter has failed in the worst way. Better a broken ankle than a broken skull.
2. *Steer the boulderer toward a good landing.* By steering the falling climber toward a good landing the spotter

"...center of gravity..."

RIGHT

Scott Blunk properly spotting Chris Jones in Rocky Mountain National Park. Scott's eyes are focused on Chris's center of gravity. When Chris's left hand came off, his center of gravity dropped quickly. Seeing this, Scott grabs Chris by the waist and steers him to a safe landing.

protects the boulderer's ankles, knees, etc.

3. *Break the boulderer's fall.* By absorbing some of the force of a fall, the spotter lessens the force of the boulderer's final impact.

4. *Do not interfere with the ascent.* The spotter should interfere with the fall, not the ascent. Avoid touching a boulderer while he or she is climbing.

Watching The Climber

When spotting, focus on the boulderer's center of gravity. With most men this is a few inches above the belt line. With most females, it is at the belt line. If you see this point rapidly dropping, then the boulderer is surely falling and it's time to do your thing. Many spotters make the mistake of watching the hands, arms, feet, or legs. These have a tendency to fly about and give the appearance that the climber is falling, when really he or she is still hanging on and busting a nut (or an ovary) trying to send the problem. If you grab the person at this point he or she will doubtless be upset and bust you in the reproductive units. Just because a hand doesn't hit the hold it was shooting for does not automatically mean the climber will fall. The temptation to watch hands and feet to discover sequences is great, but if you want to do that, do your partner a favor and let somebody else spot.

When watching the boulderer, try to establish a sense for which way he or she might fall from any given move. If he or she doesn't discuss probable falling angles, don't be afraid to ask the boulderer where he or she expects to fall from, and where is the anticipated landing. Even with these clues, one must still be alert at all times. Unexpected falls are often the worst.

Making The Catch

In most situations, the spotter will actually grab hold of the falling boulderer to break the fall and steer the body to a good landing. When falling from vertical or less-than-vertical terrain, the boulderer's body will usually be aligned vertically, heading toward the ground feet-first. In this case, grab the boulderer by the hips and steer toward a good landing. Absorb some of the fall with your arms and legs. Let the boulderer absorb the rest of the fall with his or her legs when hitting the ground. Keep hold of the boulderer, if possible, so he or she doesn't roll away after landing. A climber's worst injuries may come not from the initial impact, but from impacts taken while rolling.

When one is climbing overhangs or falling over backwards (say due to a snapped layaway hold) the body often falls at an angle to the ground, instead of feet-first. Sometimes it can even go head-first. In these hazardous cases grab farther up the body (above the center of gravity), along the upper lats or in the armpits. This will cause the body to rotate feet-downwards. Steer the climber to a good landing and absorb the impact as above.

The Bump-And-Catch

This is a more advanced technique than those above, but has the advantage of absorbing a lot of fall force. It is a good technique for spotting long falls or for people spotting boulderers larger than themselves. This should only be done when the climber is falling feet-first. When the boulderer comes toward you, hit the boulderer's buttocks with the palms of your hands like you're setting a 200-pound volleyball. This should absorb much of the speed and force of the fall. Done correctly, the boulderer will slow down and you can quickly grab the hips and steer toward a good landing. Done incorrectly and it can cause the climber to flip over backwards on top of you—a dangerous situation for all parties concerned. Practice this with a backup spotter.

Shoving

In some situations, the best a spotter can offer is a redirection of the falling boulderer's trajectory away from a hazard. In this case the spot consists of a quick shove away from the hazard and toward a better landing. The falling boulderer is then responsible for breaking the rest of his or her fall. This may involve rolling. Often a bump-and-catch is more like a bump-and-shove.

Gang Spots

This is when more than one spotter is watching the boulderer. If coordinated well, a whole gang of spotters can be more effective than a single great spotter. This is a good tactic when there are multiple hazards to contend with. All spotters must be clear as to what their assignments are. Let's say Latrina is climbing. Joe, being light but quick, is in charge of shoving her away from the broken branches on the right. Manuel, because of his surefootedness, stands on the slab to the left and keeps her from falling in the Indian grinding holes. Bertha, a trigonometry major, tends the sketchpad and moves it between potential landing zones as Latrina moves out the roof. And Bubba, being state power lifting champ, is in charge of the final catch. Be sure to discuss who will do what before someone falls. Two spotters getting in each other's way can lead to more injuries than if there were no spot at all.

"Is that the right foothold?"

WRONG

Name Withheld (NW) suffers a momentary lapse while spotting Ed Van Steenwyk on Bitch Rock, Cradlerock, New Jersey. NW is too busy looking at Ed's foot and/or pointing out a toehold. If Ed's fingers rip loose, he will hurtle past NW to the right. NW's right hand is too far left to stop such a fall, and he might or might not make the catch with his left. The best way to handle such a situation? Memorize the footholds before leaving the ground, so your spotter can concentrate on spotting.

The boulderer is falling off "Cocaine Corner," a scary problem in Yosemite. Adam Massey straddles a nasty block and shoves the boulderer away from it and toward the sketchpad. Without the spot, the climber may well have broken his legs.

Nick Papa gets a gang spot on "The Morgue," Hueco Tanks. Several large rocks clutter the path under the roof, creating a bad landing and making it hard for the spotter to follow. The two spotters leap frog each other, one spotting while the other moves to the next position. The foreground spotter is watching Nick's hand jams, and in this case, may be excused for not watching Nick's center of gravity. If Nick's hands slip out of the crack, he will fall head first; if his feet squirt out, they'll swing safely to the ground. Even though the spotter is ready for the worst case scenario (hands ripping), he'd get the same warning by focusing on Nick's center of gravity. What's more, he'd be better able to grab Nick's armpits to break his fall.

Spotting Beta

It is a good idea to plan a spotting sequence for each problem. On a simple straight-up problem, the spotter might never change stances. On traverses and overhangs, the spotter might move many times. These moves may require negotiating obstacles such as boulders, bushes, tree roots, or street curbs. Know what is underfoot so you don't trip and fall. Plan the moves between stances so you can move when the boulderer is least likely to fall and need your services. Practice these moves between stances so you can switch positions quickly. If you are gang spotting, you can leapfrog between stances and never leave the boulderer unprotected. Know at each point in the problem which way you will direct a fall.

Calling Off The Spot

Sooner or later some psycho will talk you into spotting him or her on a ridiculous problem. Before you know it, the climber's feet are fifteen feet up, knees doing the Elvis, and the confident, challenging voice that coaxed you into this has turned into a high-pitched whimper. If there is a fall, you will end up two feet shorter. When you put yourself in as much danger as the climber you're spotting, you have every right to call off the spot. The high boulderer may not like this, but understands it's part of the game. Ideally you will explain the situation before he or she starts up the problem: "I'll spot you until you reach that mantel, then you're on your own," or even just, "I might have to bail on you if you get too high for my spotting ability. I'll yell if I'm chickening out." What is inexcusable is to leave your post without warning the climber. This is a violation of the sacred trust. I've topped out on more than one tall problem not to be elated at succeeding, but to be pissed because my spotter had vamoosed without telling me.

SKETCHPAD USE

It's funny that modern bouldering—which is essentially gymnastics using boulders for appa- ratus—quickly borrowed dynamic moves and spotting from gymnastics, but was slow to incorporate padded landings. In the old days, we'd pad a sharp stone or a tree root with a pack or a sweater. In the extreme case in Yosemite in the '70s, climbers pilfered mattresses from

Even covered with a sketchpad, this unassuming root could seriously twist an ankle of landed upon, hence, I mark a "no-fall zone" on my sketch pad.

employee dorms, then dragged them over to the Camp 4 boulders to cover the jagged blocks under Bachar Cracker. Nevertheless, portable, custom-made pads didn't arrive on the scene until around 1990, over 30 years after the advent of gymnastic bouldering.

Proper placement of your sketchpad is most important. Three years ago I took a mere four-foot hop off some pissy variant to an otherwise easy problem on Mount Sanitas, in Colorado. I landed on my sketchpad with all of my right foot and the heel of my left foot. The ball of my left foot hit a wal- nut-sized stone and I broke the peanut-sized sesmoid bones that protect that joint. Today, that foot still gives me problems. Sketchpads don't work if you don't hit them.

Some people make the mistake of leaving the pad at the base of the first moves, so they can wipe their feet before starting. On vertical to less-than-vertical straight-up problems this will work. On overhanging, angling, or traversing prob- lems this probably won't be the case. Anticipate the most likely place you will fall and place the pad there. (See the Falling And Jumping section for advice on determining fall angles.) Use a carpet swatch to wipe your feet on.

On this freaky problem near Fort Collins, Colorado, Mark Wilford opts not to pad the landing. This rock slopes enough so that a sketchpad on top of it would skid out from under Mark's feet if he hit it, causing him to land on his face.

The most important consideration in placing a pad is where it will reduce risk of injury the most. This is not nec- essarily under the crux moves. In some cases there might be a nice cushy natural landing where you are most apt to fall, but a nest of punji sticks under the easy moves. Automatically placing the sketchpad under the most likely spot you'll fall can be a mistake. If the sketchpad can be used to protect a more hazardous landing on an easier move, and you think you can survive falls elsewhere on the problem unaided, then use the pad to reduce the risk as much as possible. Better yet, go with a buddy who has a pad too, and cover all the hazards.

Tommy Herbert nails the famous lightning bolt hold on "Midnight Lightning," Yosemite. Sticking this hold and matching on it is considered by many to be the crux. If Tommy falls now, he will miss the sketchpad. This is intentional: he has placed the pad over the granite slab under the lip moves (also hard). In this way, he protects against a longer fall onto a harder landing.

Bring the biggest pad you are willing to carry. On steep, slabby landings the pad may try to slide out of position. Flip the sketchpad upside-down so the higher- friction fleece side contacts the slab. If this doesn't stop the sliding, anchor the pad with the leash or another tie-down.

If you have several companions along, one can slide the sketchpad around during the course of the problem. It helps to have a four-foot or longer leash attached to the pad to drag it without having to stoop. Do a practice drag to be sure the pad doesn't snag.

In some cases an unevenness, such as an embedded stone or tree root, may lurk under only part of the pad, but you definitely want the pad covering the area surrounding it. In this case I will take a chunk of chalk and outline the "no-fall/don't land here zone" on the pad. When I jump or fall off, I will make every effort not to land in that outlined area. In some cases, the unevenness can be filled in with a pack or sweater, then the sketchpad placed on top.

When Not To Use A Sketchpad

A sketchpad may give a false sense of security on problems with a jumble of boulders or a bevy of deeply exposed tree roots at the base. The pad will look nice and cushy, but when you land it will collapse or twist around that rack of bowling balls beneath it, causing your ankle to twist or collapse as well. In these cases, I prefer to forgo the pad and rely on the "boulder run" technique instead.

When You Want One But You Ain't Got One

Do like in the old days: pad the landing with a pack or a sweater. Put your sandwich over the coat peg of rock lurking behind you. Be creative. Heck, I've even stacked cow pies over a nasty stone spicing up an otherwise grassy meadow landing.

Puppy Love

I am desperately in love with my dog, Thimble. She's the most beautiful creature in the world and I get warm and fuzzy just writing about her. This is why I absolutely refuse to let her lie down on any sketchpad or carpet—even mine—whether it's being used or not. Call it "tough love," but my dog's well-being and safety must come before her comfort. Dogs who lie on sketchpads will eventually be hit by a falling climber. I've heard of at least one canine fatality caused by a falling climber. Don't let this happen to your best friend: teach him or her that sketchpads are off-route. If need be, tie your dog up when you are bouldering, or bring your dog a separate blanket or pad to lounge on. By the way, Thimble does get to sleep on my bed.

DOWNCLIMBING

Downclimbing is one of the best ways to get out of trouble. It saves wear on the joints caused by jumping, and it is a great way to get viciously strong. The legendary Jim Holloway attributed much of his bouldering strength to the fact that he tried to downclimb nearly every problem he could climb up. Downclimbing is often the only safe course of retreat from a problem. Consequently, it is one of the foremost tools in the high boulderer's repertoire. The disadvantage to downclimbing is that it requires strength and therefore uses up energy that could be put into another attempt. Occasionally a muscle strain can occur downclimbing if one "falls" onto a hold.

DEALING WITH LOOSE ROCK

The best solution to dealing with loose holds is to learn the techniques for climbing on them. This also happens to be an indispensable skill for other types of climbing, especially soloing. Learn to evaluate holds by the sound they make when hit with the palm of your hand, rapped on with your knuckles, or kicked with your toe. Hollow sounds indicate loose holds. So can vibrations. Be suspicious of holds when you can see cracks (hairline or otherwise) surrounding the hold—even if the hold doesn't sound hollow or vibrate. Learn to pull on loose holds in the direction toward which they are supported (Photo). Don't pull out on them. Pull down (or sideways if supported from the sides and not from beneath) and push the hold against the rock. Sometimes it's better to go with a smaller solid hold and do a harder move than to risk snapping a hold.

Distribute your weight amongst several holds. In this way one can use holds that won't support full body weight. It also prepares one to catch oneself on another hold should a hold break. I tense my muscles more when climbing on loose holds so they will be prepared to instantly absorb the shock of catching full weight on a hold should another hold snap.

When you let go to reach for a hold, only one hand will be on the rock. To avoid overweighting that handhold, you can dyno to the next hold even if you could reach it statically. In this way you can generate the force for the move with your weight distributed between arms and legs. When you let go to reach up, you "float" through the instant when one hand is off the rock and consequently don't overload the loose hold your other hand is on.

A dubious, hollow-sounding flake on the Bolt Wall at Horsetooth Reservoir. Pulling outward might snap it (above), but it can be safely used by pulling straight down (below). Notice how the palm and forearm pushes the hold against the wall.

The "Gill Egg" in the Shawangunks,
New York. Dave Lanman flies for the
incut on this classic Gill problem.

The Art of Dynamic Movement

In 1958, John Gill started a revolution in rock climbing. He decided to approach rock climbing as an extension of gymnastics, rather than an extension of hiking or mountaineering. He took this new philosophy to the boulders, and actively sought out problems that could only be climbed dynamically. Hence modern bouldering was born and ever since dynamic movement has remained the soul of the sport.

STANDARD DYNAMICS

When you don't have the strength to lock off and reach a hold statically, it's time to dyno. Even if you can crank a move statically, doing it dynamically can save a lot of energy and perhaps make the difference in doing that next move. Furthermore, dynamics, when performed correctly, are kinesthetically pleasing and down-right fun. Short of skydiving, it's the closest you'll come to flying. Dynamics are most commonly used on vertical-to-overhanging rock.

Commit! Chris Jones in Montana.

Five quick rules:
- *Push with your legs, don't pull with your arms.*
- *Use your arms to pivot and direct.*
- *Crouch once, then fire—don't pump doubt.*
- *Commit.*
- *Don't overdyno.*

1. Using Your Legs
The most important thing to remember when dynoing is to propel yourself with your legs. They are much stronger than your arms and will launch you farther and save your arm strength for other moves.

Determining which footholds to push off from requires experience. The more dyno problems you do, the better you will become at judging how high or low your feet should be for a given move. In general, use the biggest footholds available so you can push off harder. If, however, the bigger footholds are awkwardly placed, say too high, too low, or staggered, you may be better off using smaller footholds that feel better. If the footholds permit, plant both feet equidistant from the hold you are shooting for. For example, if you're shooting straight up, a line drawn through both feet will be

Skip Guerin dynos up and left to start "Mongolian Cosmonaut," Flagstaff Mountain, Colorado. His right foot is higher than his left, but both feet are roughly equidistant from the target hold. His left foot pushes his body up, while his right pushes it to the left. This is the best way to set up for a sideways or angling dyno: one foot under the body to support weight and provide vertical thrust, the other to the side to provide thrust in the direction of the target hold.

parallel to the ground (assuming the ground is level); if you're dynoing sideways, the foot opposite the direction you are dynoing in will be higher than the other. This will make it easier to push off smoothly and guide your trajectory.

If you are dynoing for a hard-to-grasp hold (small, sloping, or awkwardly angled), you'll have an easier time sticking it if your feet don't come off the rock. Keeping your feet on the rock will help kill any barndoor effect and will also take some of your body weight. Given multiple footholds of equal size to choose from, I pick the lowest set that my feet will stay on when I hit the hold I'm shooting for. (See Sizing Up A Move in Chapter 5.)

There is a point of diminishing returns as you bring your feet higher and higher up the rock to do a dyno. This point varies from individual to individual, depending on leg strength and flexibility, but most folks will find it hard to push off their feet if they are placed any higher than their hips. Practice is the key to getting the feel for dynamics.

2. Using Your Arms

Unless you have wings instead of arms, don't use your arms to propel yourself upwards when dynoing. On a properly executed dyno, the arms are used to pivot and direct the body, not to propel it. Dynos done with the arms are usually sloppy, strength-wasting slap jobs. Done with the legs they are smooth, efficient works of art.

When dynoing, keep your arms relatively straight as you pivot about your starting handhold. The more overhanging the move, the straighter your arms can stay throughout the move. As walls get closer to vertical your arms will bend more to keep your body in close to the rock. The more overhanging the wall, the less vertical component there will be to a dyno of any given length and the greater an arc you can let your body take. On vertical walls, flatten out the arc so as to give maximum vertical component to your thrust. Use your leg power to push up, not out. Your arms will pull you in so your legs can push you up. Your arms are not pulling you up.

3. Crouch Once...Then Fire!

Sink down low enough to get the needed thrust from your legs, then fire for the hold. Exhale while you push off.

4. Commitment

Commit to the move. Imagine yourself latching that next hold with confidence. Crouch and fire like you own that move. Half-assed attempts give half-assed results.

5. Avoid Overdynoing

Only lunge as far as needed to hit the hold. Try to land on it softly, like a leaf dropping from the sky. This will make the transfer of weight to that hold easier and less likely to cause injury.

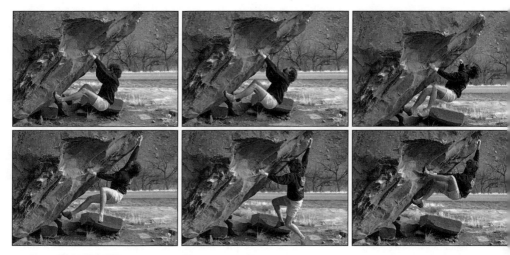

THE BIG MISTAKE

If we could harness all the energy wasted by boulderers unnecessarily pumping their bodies up and down before they lunged, we could keep the Vegas Strip lit up year-round for free. Many boulderers use a "One…two…three…Go!" series of body thrusts before they actually take off for the hold. They justify this as "psyching up" and "building rhythm." More likely they are psyching out and wasting strength. I call this "pumping doubt." The proper place to psych for the dyno is not bobbing up and down on the holds, but at the base of the problem before you step off the ground. Heck, why not psych up the night before while you're doing the dishes. When you get to the move, crouch down once and fire. You'll be blown away how much easier it is. Basically, if you pump three times before you shoot, you could have just tried the problem three times.

Four Cases Where An Extra Thrust Won't Hurt

Nine out of ten times, extra pumps are a big blunder. There are, however, four special cases where it isn't.

On your first time up a problem, an extra pump can be the right thing to do. It can give you a preview of how the move will feel. You might judge the distance to the next hold better or get some balance clues. You might decide you want to launch from different footholds. Once you've had your preview though, it's time to get down to business—crouch once and fire. On subsequent attempts, forgo the pre-pump—again, crouch once and fire.

Case two exists on really long dynos where you need maximum thrust and your legs fold up completely, butt-to-heels, before you launch. In this case take advantage of the stretch reflex. This is the little bounce you get when you squat down quickly, maxing out that range of motion. Your body senses

On a dyno at Big Bend Boulder near Moab, Utah, I set my feet, crouch, then blast for the lip. My arm stays straight as I pivot around the starting handhold, the thrust for the dyno comes from my legs. Both feet come off when I catch the lip, so I have to hang tight with my left hand to keep myself from swinging off.

The author on some obscure hunkpile behind his house. His feet are perched on tiny holds at the same level. He could place his left foot higher up on a larger hold, but it would create an awkward push-off.

Variation on Pitch Penny Boulder, Horsetooth Reservoir. When doing vertical dynos, the arms bend, not to pull one upwards, but to pull the body over the feet so the legs can push you straight up. Here I get set, crouch once, then push upward. In the fourth photo, my feet have just left the footholds as my left hand releases to reach upward. My right hand still guides the dyno, but all the vertical thrust has come from my legs. The target knob is a few inches right of the holds I took off from, so when I catch it in the last photo, it causes my body to barndoor slightly right. Though my right foot looks like it's pushing off a small hold in the last photo, it is actually kicking into the wall to control this barndoor.

this, and bounces you back up a few degrees to ease the stress. Use this bounce to initiate a more powerful deep leg thrust. Often you can get the bounce by just crouching down quickly, but sometimes a short pump upwards followed by a quick drop gives a better bounce.

Case three occurs on roofs and very steep overhangs. On these it's hard to get into a crouched position before you fire. When you try to crouch down, your butt just drops towards the ground, not toward your feet. Push your legs straight once, then let your body pivot back downwards. The momentum it has will carry your center of gravity past the low point of the arc and back up toward your feet into a crouched position. When it reaches this position, push off on the footholds and blast toward the next hold. Usually one pump is enough to get into a deep enough crouch, but sometimes it may take another pump or two, each time increasing the length of the arc. Sometimes a toehook can pull one into the crouched position, eliminating the need for the extra pump, but forcing one then to push off from one foot alone.

Case four happens when dynoing sideways and you can't position your feet to push in the direction you want to go. For example, your hands are matched on a jug and you want to dyno five feet straight right for another jug. You wish there were footholds to your left to push off from, but the only footholds are directly beneath your hands. To get the momentum to reach right, swing your body from side to side (right-to-left and back) several times until you generate enough momentum to reach the next hold. (See photos on p. 31.)

DOUBLE DYNOS

Double dynos are dynamic moves where both hands (and usually both feet) come off the rock. This usually happens when the handholds are spaced more than an arm span apart. As with other dynos, provide most of the thrust with the legs and use the arms more as pivot points. Commitment is the key to double dynos, as you cannot reverse such a move.

SWING STARTS

There is no rule stating that you cannot jump for the first holds on a problem. Sometimes this is as simple as just crouching down and jumping up to the first holds. When those holds are too small or far away to grab this way, the swing start comes into play.

Swing starts were a John Gill favorite and a technique I like a lot too. It consists of putting one hand on the rock, then dynoing from the ground to a hold high up the wall. Both feet can push off the ground or one foot can push off the ground and the other off the rock. Use the handhold as a barely weighted pivot point to help direct the dyno: or, if big enough, pull on it to help launch the body up. A lot of my friends pooh-pooh swing starts, saying you must start all problems with both feet on the rock. Had I held this belief myself, I would have missed out on many excellent problems. I find that the climbers who denigrate this technique are invariably piss poor at it. It's not as easy as it sounds.

Like any dyno, the thrust for a swing start should come mainly from the legs. Use the hand on the rock mostly as a pivot. Crouch down and explode up. Only crouch once—no "pumping doubt." To gain added height on a swing start, drop your free hand low as you crouch. When you dyno, swing that arm upwards toward the high hold. This arm swing will provide more upward momentum. (To check this at home, do a vertical leap starting with your hands above your head. Now try it starting with both hands low and swinging them up as you leap.)

Because you only have one hand and one or no feet on the rock during a swing start, barndooring can easily happen. The trick to swing starts is to control or eliminate this barndoor. To do this, pick the launch spot for your foot or feet carefully; sometimes moving your foot just an inch to the side can make a dramatic difference. Often, one must try several different launch spots to find the best one. Before you blast off, mark the spot you took off from by scratching a line to the tip of your toe in the dirt or by positioning your carpet so you take off from one corner. If you launch with success, but fail higher on the problem, it might take you several more tries to find an unmarked take-off spot again.

Sometimes barndooring can't be eliminated. When barndooring is a problem, it is usually because the climber's body barndoors away from the rock at the moment the climber grasps the high hold. To fight this tendency, you can start with your feet positioned such as to initiate a subtle barndooring into the rock. This usually involves positioning your feet

On this contrivance, I want to dyno for a hold five feet to my right, just left of the crack. However, I don't have any footholds to my left to push off from. To get momentum for the move, I swing right, then left, then back right again. Were I dynoing all the way to the crack, I might have to swing side to side again to get the necessary momentum.

In 1958, John Gill fired this outrageous swing start at Wyoming's Jenny Lake Boulders, thus ushering in the age of modern dynamic bouldering. Thirty years later, I found it was still desperate to stick the hidden bottle-cap sized hold at the lip. It took me many tries to find the perfect spot on the ground to launch from.

Nowhere in the Ten Commandments does it state "Thou shalt not jump for the first holds." Matt Brotherton attempts "Arabesque," Dixon Springs, Illinois.

farther away from the base. These moves often feel awkward when one sets up, but halfway through the move, the body ends up taking a more favorable trajectory, ending with a soft landing on the target hold. If your body is still swinging in when you latch the hold, you stand a better chance of hanging on than if your body were swinging out at that moment. If you over-do this, however, your body will swing back out after you've latched the hold and could pull you off. The key is to make this inwards barndoor very subtle so that it cancels itself at the top of the move.

Another way to control barndooring is to vary the angle of your arm swing. This can cause your body to barndoor one way or the other, even if your feet take off from the same spot. You can change the angle of your arm swing to adjust how much you barndoor. Practice with different angles of arm swing. Practicing swing starts can be a great way to learn how your body moves during dynos. This knowledge can then be used on all dynos, whether they start from the ground, or higher, off the deck.

Swing starts take a lot of practice to get good at. No matter how good you are, there will always be a problem out there you can start no other way. When you stick one there is an instant feeling of kinesthetic awareness that is a wonderful way to start a problem. Some people would rather use cheater stones than do a swing start. These poor chumps are missing out on some of the coolest moves out there.

LINKED DYNAMICS

Just as a gymnast can use the momentum from one dynamic move to initiate the next dynamic move, so can a boulderer. Gill once wrote about this as being a potential future direction for bouldering. He was doubtless influenced by his rope climbing (a former event in gymnastics meets) in which the momentum of a powerful start could be maintained to the top of the 20-foot rope. (From a sit-down start, Gill could climb the rope in 3.4 seconds.) Because speed is rarely pursued in bouldering, and it is rarely necessary to climb problems fast (other than forearm-melting traverses), the concept of linked dynamics has not been carried very far. I can think of three situations where this conservation of momentum comes in useful.

The first is dynamics, in which the feet start from greatly differing heights. A common example is a swing start with one foot on the ground and one foot high on the rock, say about waist level. Initially the foot on the rock is too high to push off of. Hence, the foot on the ground provides the initial momentum. When the body rises high enough, the foot on the rock starts pushing, propelling the body much further up

the rock than if both feet had started on the ground. Less common are dynos starting with both feet on the rock, but at greatly differing heights. In reality, any dyno starting without the legs evenly extended will apply this conservation of momentum principle when weight shifts from one leg to the other. However, it is most noticeable when the leg thrusts are spaced further apart.

The second linked-dynamic situation is on no-foot traverses: for example, traversing the lip of a roof. If one's hands

Using a swing start to do Pinch Overhand, a Gill classic on the Mental Block at Horsetooth Reservoir. Note how the free arm starts low then swings up for added momentum. (See p.31)

shuffle so quickly along the lip that one's body trails the hands, the momentum of the body trying to swing and catch up with the hands can propel the climber across the traverse. To experience this, find a steel I-beam beneath a ceiling, a fat doorjamb across a garage door, or the continuous horizontal rail on a jungle-gym ladder. Traverse as fast as you can with your legs dangling. As long as your feet trail your hands you will fly across. As soon as your legs start swinging back and forth you will slow down. If you're strong enough, most problems suited to linked-dynamic traversing will succumb without this technique. However, linked dynamics give tremendous kinesthetic pleasure. The classic Nat's Traverse at Mortar Rock in Berkeley has a ten-foot leg-dangling section that is much more fun when done in one uninterrupted linked-dynamic flow.

The third variation on the linked dynamic theme is the run-and-jump. This consists of running up to a boulder, jumping off the ground, kicking off the rock with one foot and latching the target hold—all in one uninterrupted sequence. These problems can be great fun and can sometimes consist of several kicks up a face before the hands ever touch. Joshua Tree National Monument is famous for its run-and-jumps. Locals have even devised a rating scheme (J ratings) to compare the difficulty of the jump problems there.

Theoretically, one could dyno upwards, catch a hold, pull on it immediately and keep dynoing upward utilizing the momentum from the first move. While this sounds appealing,

Above: Kipping with the legs to do the no-foot dyno on Gill's "Juggernaut," near Pueblo, Colorado.

Right: The no-foot linked dynamic sequence on "Nat's Traverse," Mortar Rock, Berkeley, California.

#1

#2

#3

#4

#5

#6

in practice it is nearly impossible to find a problem that can only be done that way.

FEET-OFF DYNOS

At some point you might find yourself dangling from holds, unable to get your feet on the rock. If you hadn't kicked everyone's butt in a one-arm pull-up contest that morning, you'd just lock the next move off.

Unfortunately, locking off at your nipple ain't happening so you're forced to lunge. No doubt about it, big guns help here, but you can still get help from your legs by kipping. Kipping is a quick raising of the legs, usually into a sitting or L-position. For an instant, the momentum from the kip takes some of the weight off your arms. At this instant, pull up for all you're worth and snag the next hold. The resultant bend at your waist also makes more muscle groups available to help the arms pull up. One can also swing one's body back and forth like a pendulum and at the high point of the arc add a kip and fire. You can practice these moves on a pull-up bar.

On no-foot traverse moves, you can sometimes find yourself stuck in an iron-cross position, unable to let go to match on the hold you just grabbed. Your feet are dangling straight below you, and you feel that if you let go with one hand you'll drop on the other arm and rip it from your shoulder like a weed being pulled. To get out of this situation, swing your legs from side to side. As your feet come up under the hand you want to release, you will feel the weight come off that hand. At this momentary "deadpoint," let go of the hold and match hands. Hang on tight when your legs swing back down. This is easily practiced on a wide pull-up bar.

Frank DiSanto sets up for a long dyno at Howard's Knob, North Carolina. Initially his right foot is too high to push with, so he needs a two-stage approach. He must use his left foot to propel his body up and onto his right foot, then push like crazy with his right foot to fly to the target hold.

Tommy Herbert at the Bachar Boulders,
north of Mammoth Lakes, California.

CHAPTER 4

Finesse and Power

Bouldering is more than just throwing dynamics. Slowly powering through a move or delicately dancing up a slab can be just as rewarding; so, too, can be cruising up a rare boulder crack. Finesse depends on well-practiced technique and a calm mind. Power is dependent on strength and using the right muscles. For optimum results the two should go hand-in-hand.

FOOTWORK

A few years ago some famous European boulderers created a splash at Hueco Tanks. Many of my fellow Americans were agog at how strong they were. Personally, I felt I knew many boulderers whose fingers and arms were just as strong. What blew me away was how precisely these Euros used their feet. Shame dealt me a low blow when I compared my own foot-work to theirs. It was obvious that these guys had spent a lot of time perfecting their footwork. One of the best ways to look outrageously powerful is to use your feet well. Footwork is the key to finesse. Precision, Trust, and Practice are the keys to good footwork.

Precision

Keep your eyes on your feet until you paste them onto the holds. Usually, a climber looks away from a foothold the second before touching a foot to it. Then he or she wiggles the foot around on the hold trying to get better purchase. By watching your foot as it settles on the hold, you will have more precise footwork, which means less time getting tired while your feet are dicking around.

Trust

Weight your feet and trust them. More weight on your feet makes your shoes stick to the rock better. It also means less weight on your arms so more power is saved for harder moves. Practice weighting your feet by consciously trying to do problems with as little support from your arms as possible. Find an easy problem and climb it with just your feet and your thumbs. Try doing problems one-handed or sans hands. Fool around at the base of a boulder trying to stand on the smallest hold possible.

Practice

It's easy to get in a rut of only trying spectacular power problems and ignoring slabs. Micro-edge slab climbing, however,

Trust those feet to support your weight. Roland Foster bouldering by the Arkansas River, Colorado.

(From top to bottom)

Steve Moyles Climbing "Falling Ant Slab" no-handed, Jenny Lake Boulders.

"Over Yourself," Flagstaff Mountain, Colorado. Skip Guerin turns sideways to keep his hips into the rock and his weight over his feet.

Heels low and "nose over toes," Eve Tallman uses good smearing technique at Lumpy Ridge, Colorado.

does wonders for your footwork. Practice standing on all parts of your feet: inside toe, outside toe, heel—even arch smears on arêtes. This practice will pay off later on the power problems.

BREATHING

Don't forget to breathe while you're on a problem. This sounds simple, but it happens all the time. Exhale during hard moves and dynamics, just as a weight lifter exhales when pressing a barbell. Take deep breaths to calm yourself when the going gets scary.

VERTICAL & LESS-THAN-VERTICAL FACES

The key on these is to stay on your feet. On vertical terrain, try to keep your hips in close to the rock—good hip turnout helps here. If your hip turnout is poor, you can align your body sideways to the rock to keep one hip in. This usually requires you to stand on the outside of one foot. On less-than-vertical walls, keep your "nose over your toes" and keep your heels low to force more rubber onto the rock. Don't lean in to the rock or stand on tippy-toes— your feet will skate out from under you, unless they are placed on positive edges.

OVERHANGING FACE TECHNIQUE

When the rock overhangs, power becomes increasingly important. Attaining power is simply a matter of climbing lots of strenuous problems and/or putting in tons of gym time. The biggest mistake most boulderers make on overhanging stone is trying to use all power and no finesse. When you're climbing at your limit you need both. Dynamic moves have already been discussed. Following are some additional tips for when the going gets steep:

- *Keep your weight on your feet.*
- *Take advantage of heel hooks, knee bars, and oppositions.*
- *Keep your arms straight whenever possible.*
- *Use big muscles instead of arms.*
- *Plan rests in advance and move fast between them.*

Feet, Feet, Feet

Repeat after me: "I will put as much weight on my feet as possible at all times, especially on overhangs." Overhangs force weight onto your arms. The steeper the terrain, the quicker the clock is ticking toward ultimate forearm melt-down. To slow the clock, put as much weight on your feet as possible. On overhangs this takes great abdominal strength. On overhangs up to 120 degrees, try keeping your hips in close to the rock to force weight on your feet. High footholds

can work well because they provide a support point closer to your center of gravity. Sometimes you can step up on a waist-high hold and sit on your heel. This takes a lot of weight off your arms, allowing you to utilize smaller fingerholds.

Heels, Knees, And Oppositions

When it gets steeper than 120 degrees, it's often easier to weight your feet by hooking your heel on a hold above your center of gravity. Frequently, a heel is hooked even with or above one's hands. If you can find a heel-toe jam, so much the better. Between 90 and 120 degrees, hooking a heel below one's center of gravity can work well, provided the hook is positive enough to resist an outward pull.

Knee bars can make the difference between spitting blood on the crux or letting go on the same move to sign auto-graphs. Look for them before you go up on a problem. Even if your knee does not lock into a bar, it can be "scummed" against the rock to take some weight off your hands.

Drop-knee technique works well on overhanging walls with footholds one can stem between. It gets the feet high and the hips close to the rock. This posture puts your center of gravity close to your feet, putting more weight on your feet and less on your arms. The body is oriented sideways to the wall. The leg in front of you is straight or nearly so, while the leg behind you pushes off a high hold with the knee bent sharply and pointing down. Often the dropped knee is lower

(Clockwise from left)

Mari Gingery smears high with her left foot to take weight off her fingers. Her right leg is "flagged," serving as a counterbalance to let her move her right hand up without barndooring.

Tommy Herbert uses a high foothold to force as much weight as possible onto his feet, "High Plains Drifter," Buttermilk, California.

"The Devil In Chris Jones," Hueco Tanks. Here I push with my left foot to keep my right toehook weighted so it doesn't fall out. On their own, neither of these feet would stay put, in opposition they do.

than the foot. Reaches from this position are usually done with the arm from the same side as the knee that is dropped.

Oppositions occur whenever two body parts push in different directions to hold one in place. The most common are stems, drop knees, liebacks, underclings and chimney techniques, but you can and should be creative. Sticking to the undersides of roofs usually involves oppositions, particularly toehooks. One can push off one foot and hook the opposite toe to keep it on, or just undercling with the toe in opposition to a hand pulling down. Toehooking usually takes lots of abdominal strength.

Straight-Arm It

Keep arms as straight as possible. Allow your skeleton to support your weight, not your muscles. When moving up, use your legs to push your weight up. The arms are only there to hold your body in. Only bend them when necessary. If you can't hang straight-armed to rest, try to get into a full lock-off position with hand next to shoulder and chest sucked into the wall. This is the next most restful position.

On horizontal roofs your arms don't need to pull up. Keep them straight and move between holds as if you were on a set of monkey bars. Use heel- and toehooks to take weight off your fingers.

Body Twists

On severely overhanging rock, one can progress between holds with body twists while still keeping one's arms fairly straight. Your torso muscles are bigger and more powerful than your arms. Use those torso muscles to twist your upper body so the shoulder axis becomes perpendicular to the rock. Your supporting arm remains straight and is crossing your chest and stomach. You'll be amazed at how far you can now reach up with your free hand.

(From top to bottom)

"Helicopter," Morrison, Colorado. Hillary Harris using a heel hook to take as much weight off her arms as possible. She also saves strength by keeping her arms straight.

A knee bar rest, Hueco Tanks.

Michelle Hurni doing a drop knee.

RESTING

Many boulder problems will have no rests, so it's up to you to sprint for the finish. However, there are some mighty long traverses and roofs out there where you won't stand a chance if you don't rest. Plan where you will rest in advance. Look for spots with big footholds, huge handholds, knee bars, over-the-head heel-toe locks, good jams, and so forth. A good kneebar is usually your best bet, but again, be creative. One time on a 50-foot roof, I copped a crucial rest in a five-foot diameter pod by stemming my feet out on one wall and pressing the top of my head against a scoop in the opposite wall. I was facing straight down with arms dangling free and my butt sticking up like a stink beetle. It was uncomfortable, but it worked.

Move fast between rests.

CRACKS

Most boulders are solid chunks of stone devoid of cracks, but sometimes you'll get lucky and find a juicy jam crack splitting a boulder. Crack climbs on cliffs are usually hard because they're long and continuous and you have to hang on to place gear. Cracks in boulders are usually short and are only hard if they are a bad size, greatly flared, or super steep. The plethora of jamming techniques is worthy of a book on it's own. In crack climbing, every ounce of technique is worth a ton of strength. A good way to practice jamming technique on boulders is to walk your hands up the crack as you climb, placing each jam immediately above the previous jam. In this fashion, you can get as many moves from a 15-foot crack as from an 80-foot long crack jammed with long reaches. By walking your hands, you don't reach past the awkward sizes and are forced to jam all the bad sizes a crack has to offer. This does wonders for your technique. It was practice like this on *Bachar Cracker* (a famous Yosemite boulder crack) that allowed me to put up problems like *Mother of the Future,*

(From left to right)

By twisting his torso, Donny Hardin uses his strong torso muscles to power up "Texas Medicine" (aka "Center El Murray") Hueco Tanks.

By keeping his arms straight and using his bare toes like fingers, Bob Murray saves his phenomenal arm power for the hard moves at Box Canyon, Socorro, New Mexico.

Mike Waugh rests with double heel-toe locks on "Hot Tuna," Stoney Point, California.

On a long traverse at Rocktown, Georgia, Rob Robinson rests his fingers by hooking his left wrist over a knob and jamming his right hand.

"The Torcher," Franconia Notch,
New Hampshire.

a 30-foot horizontal roof split by a finger- and thin-hand crack.

The various positions the hands adopt for different sizes of cracks are too great to list. Still, some mention should be given to foot jamming. Foot jams come in handy whenever there's a groove your toe can fit in. They can be used in flares too wide to jam with the hands. Often you can find a foot jam on a problem with no other jams. The common mistake I see many climbers make is just stabbing the foot straight into a crack instead of torquing it in. To foot jam properly, stuff your toes in parallel to the crack as deep as your boot will go. To do this, your knee will angle to the side of the crack. Next, apply torque by aligning your knee with the crack. This may be painful to the toes, but it is very secure and you can put much more weight on your feet this way.

PURE POWER

The techniques discussed all help take weight off the arms on steep rock. Nevertheless, you will have to pull up on your arms frequently. Use finesse to save your strength for these moves. After the power moves, get your weight back on your feet as soon as possible.

Good ways to train for power are to get on familiar problems and try to do moves statically that you normally do dynamically, or try to statically crank past holds you would normally use.

WRONG

Sloppy toe jam.

RIGHT

Good toe jam—stuffed and torqued.

Wallace Stasick approaching the crux on "Germ Free Adolescence," Eldorado Canyon, Colorado.

CHAPTER 5

More Bouldering Tricks

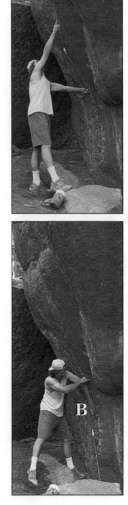

SIZING UP A MOVE

Lots of moves can be harder or easier depending on how they fit your body. Before wasting energy trying a body-size dependent sequence that may or may not work for you, measure the rock to see if you will fit. Here are three examples.

Knee bars can be great energy savers, especially on really steep problems—like those at Hueco Tanks. On my body, the distance from my fingertips to my elbow is the same as from my toes to my knee. I can hold my forearm up against a potential knee bar and know instantly if my lower leg will be too long, too short, or just right to try a knee bar. If there are several foot placements on a potential kneebar, I can find the best one with this trick. If I can't reach the area I'm sizing up, I can measure with a long stick marked with my toe-to-knee distance.

On dynos, I like to know if I can hit the target hold with my feet still on the holds they push from, or if my feet will have to come off the starter holds. (Keeping my feet on can help tremendously with my balance when I hit the target. Also, if your feet come off it will be nearly impossible to reverse the move if you miss the target hold. On feet-off lunges you generally fall further out from the face as well.) My bubbabrush (See p. 49), from the end of the blow tube to the tip of the toothbrush, is the same distance as from my knees to my fingers (held above my head). I reach my bubbabrush up to the target hold (and clean it off, of course), then hold the shaft against the rock. I make a mental note where the end of the blow tube reaches. I put my fingertips at that point then check if my elbow reaches the foothold as if measuring for a knee bar. If so, I can count on hitting the target hold with my foot still on. If not, I will plan to lunge with my feet coming off or I will pick a higher foothold, if available, to lunge from.

For heel-toe jams, I can take my boot off and check the fit. Your foot will bend in most heel-toe jams (especially with softer shoes) so if the jam is a half-inch or inch shorter than your boot, it will probably work.

I want to find the lowest foothold I can use for a dyno to handhold A and still keep my foot on. Instead of wasting energy trying the move from different holds, I measure the move and choose hold B.

Tommy Herbert chalking up on "Midnight Lightning," Yosemite, California.

USING CHALK

The use of chalk to keep hands dry is acceptable in most bouldering areas in America. Nevertheless, there are some areas in which it is not allowed, either through local consensus or statute. Before you reach into your chalk bag, be sure chalk use is acceptable where you are climbing. That said, lets dip into this subject further.

For the most part, there's nothing more to chalk use than dipping into your chalk bag whenever your hands feel moist. Occasionally, a bizarre move will be easier if you chalk up body parts other than your hands. For instance, if you're palming a rounded ledge shaped like a car fender, it may help to chalk your forearms for added friction. Or, say you're smearing your calf around an arête to stay in balance—go ahead and chalk your calf if it will help.

On really long problems on really hot days, you may want to put on a "primer coat." To do this, rub your hands together with chalk, being sure to get a good even coat, not just on the inside of the fingers, but between the fingers, across the palm and even along the backs (tops) of the fingers. I feel this chalk helps keep perspiration from creeping between the fingers and onto the inside where they contact the rock. After applying the primer coat, I sometimes chalk my tips one more time before getting on the rock. This is something to do only when you are sweating profusely and on a problem that will take several minutes or more to climb.

Gauge your chalk use according to conditions. Don't use more chalk than you need. You'll just be pissing away your money and creating a mess to boot.

What To Do When You Can't Chalk Up

Let's say you're on a problem that is long enough to exhaust the chalk you put on at the base. The climb is so hard that you're about to have an aneurysm while you desperately hang on with one hand and try to chalk up the other. Problem is you're playing hide-and-go-seek with your chalk bag that has slid around your belt and is just out of reach. Meanwhile your fingers are dripping off the holds like fudge rolling down a sundae. What do you do? Below are several strategies.

Plan A Wear double chalk bags—one on each hip. You can dip very fast this way because you aren't fishing around for a bag dangling somewhere behind your butt.

Plan B Wipe your fingers quickly across your shirt, shorts, or pants and gain some relief that way. This is much quicker than reaching into a chalk bag, even double bags, but does not have as great a drying effect unless you utilize Plan C.

Plan C Just prior to the attempt, rub a block of chalk on your shirt, arm, or back of your hand, leaving a deposit of chalk. You can quickly slap this chalky patch to dry your hands. If you have hairy arms you can store quite a bit of chalk this way. If you sweat enough to soak up the deposit of reserve chalk, or if you have the verve to shave your arms to accentuate your muscle definition, this trick may backfire. In this case, try Plan D.

Plan D Seed some of the bigger holds on the problem with sprinkled-on chalk. When you grab these holds your fingers will get a free chalk-up. Unfortunately, by sprinkling chalk on the holds, you will make them harder to hang on to (you have just defeated the purpose of cleaning them off). This is why it is best to only seed holds which are big enough that you will have no trouble hanging on whether they are clean or not.

Plan E Wait for a drier day or until you are stronger.

Ego-swelling Combat Tale #4: The First Flash of Autobahn

I include this story not just to pump up my ego—my head will probably not fit through a standard doorway after I write this—but also to give an example of the worst-case scenario when it comes to battling sweat.

Spanning 850 feet, the Autobahn is the longest bouldering traverse I know of in the U.S. It's situated in Chandler Park, overlooking Tulsa, Oklahoma. The first time I visited Chandler, the Autobahn was soaking wet in several sections. Locals told me nobody had ever flashed it. Into my mind seeped the thought of all the free beers and notoriety I would receive should I pull off this feat. Therefore, as the route was out of condition, I stayed off of any section of it, saving it for a later flash attempt.

My chance came over a year later, when I visited Tulsa one July to give a slide show. As is typical in Tulsa in midsummer, the temperature was in the mid-'90s and the Weather Channel reported 1000% (sic) humidity. Just stepping out of an air-conditioned car would cause sweat to instantly bead up on your skin. These were less than ideal conditions, but this time the route was dry and I had no idea when I would be through Tulsa again. Had I read my own book, Stone Crusade, I would have been reminded that the Tulsa hardcores (namely, anyone crazy enough to go bouldering there in the summer) wore dishtowels tucked into their shorts to dry their hands on and terry cloth tennis wristbands to intercept the streams of sweat running along their arms. Stupidly, I got on the Autobahn armed only with my standard western U.S. summer wear: double chalk bags, shoes, shorts, and a tank top. At least I had the foresight to top off my chalk bags before I started.

The first 200 feet went well and quickly. By dipping into my chalk bag every few moves I could stem the tide of sweat pouring out of my hands. The hint of a pump was creeping in, however, so my pace slowed to take advantage of the periodic rests. This slower pace though, meant that mere dips into the chalk bag could not keep up with the sweat. As I watched my feet step from toehold to toehold, I could see a dark line of sweat-soaked leather gradually migrate down from the top of my boot. Likewise, the sweat pouring along my arms rolled down to my hands whenever I lowered them to shake out or chalk up. For the next 100 to 200 feet I could wipe my arms on my shirt to dry them, but soon it became saturated, clinging wet and heavy on my body. At around the halfway point I was rubbing my entire arms with chalk, trying to get enough chalk in the hair to dam up the rivers of sweat coursing along them. Had it not been for several good stem rests I could not have let go to do this. Soon, however, it became apparent that two full chalk bags would not last me until the end of the traverse.

Between figuring out the moves, resting, and pacing myself for such a long problem, I had chewed up two hours by the time I reached the 500-foot mark. My spotters, who had enthusiastically followed my attempt for the first few hundred feet, had long ago moved on to problems of their own. Where the wall reached its tallest, I followed a high line with my hands twenty feet up. At this point my hands started to open up and my feet were moonwalking across the polished limestone. Only a display of grit and courage that would make Heinrich Harrer proud (or it might have been the fear of breaking both my legs on the uneven landing below) saw me through to the next big holds where I could hang on and call for help. My friend Damien came over, and as requested, placed my supply bag of chalk on the next ledge where I could drop both hands and manipulate it. There, I restocked my chalk bags and shook fresh blood into my arms. The sweat line on my shoes had nearly reached my toes. Soaked to capacity, my light cotton shorts were doing battle with the elastic holding them up. I thought better of taking my shirt off, figuring it might keep my shorts and the rock drier.

After another hour of pushing, pulling, stemming, shuffling, swinging, and sweating I came to a ledge where I could sit down. The water line on my shoes had by this time disappeared below the rands. My friends rejoined me: they had finished their bouldering session while I was still on my first problem. By this time my arms were rubbery and I feared blowing the flash on the last section. I took a long rest, peeling my shoes off and drinking from a water bottle tossed up to me. My friends were getting antsy. The encouragement for me to flash it had turned into: "Hurry up so we can get some cold ones."

On the home stretch I made some route finding blunders, but pulled through several times on moves when I thought my fingers would surely peel open. The end came sooner than I thought, but none-too-soon for my friends, who told me I'd been on the same problem for 3-½ hours.

The morals of this story? 1. Prepare before you take off: heed the example of others, particularly locals who have conditions figured out. 2. Have good friends along. 3. Determination, if strong enough, can substitute for strength. 4. Don't tell your partners where the car keys are until you're ready to leave.

HOLD CLEANING

Dirty holds are harder to pull and stand on than clean holds. Unless you're stepping up to a virgin problem, odds are you'll only be brushing off chalk and possibly some dirt. Climbing chalk loves to bond with moisture. That is why it sucks the sweat and wetness off your fingertips. Unfortunately, it has a limit to how much moisture it can absorb. The more moisture it absorbs, the greasier it feels. Hence we have to continually use fresh chalk to dry our fingers. The used-up chalk ends up caked to the handholds and will make them feel greasy if not cleaned off.

Brush dirty holds gently with a toothbrush to loosen dirt and greasy, used-up chalk. Blow the loosened dirt and chalk off the holds by mouth or with a blow tube attached to your bubbabrush. On some problems you may have to climb part way up, hang on, and clean off a key hold.

Neal Kaptain uses a bubbabrush to clean out a pocket.

Many Europeans and some Americans like to clean holds by whacking them with a towel. Other than for sweeping off leaves or pine needles, I find this to be fairly ineffective. It removes loose detritus, but does little for packed-on chalk. In some cases it even packs the chalk on thicker, making it harder to work with the true texture of the hold. Because the boulders have been good to me, I treat them as my friends. Towel-whacking seems to be a negative use of energy, promoting the "at war" with the boulders approach instead of being "at one" with the boulders.

For out-of-reach holds use a bubbabrush or reach over from the top of the problem or a nearby tree if possible. For cleaning while on a problem, use a brush attached to you with a string or gammon reel.

Don't forget to brush your footholds. This sounds simple, but you wouldn't believe how many climbers overlook this. Also, brushing footholds makes you attentive to where your feet will be placed, and this pays dividends when you get on the problem.

After you finish trying a problem, brush the holds before you leave. This is a courtesy to the next climber, who just might be you, and gives the holds time to "breathe." It may be my imagination, but holds seem easier to grab when they haven't been basting in greasy, used-up chalk for several days. You might as well have everything going in your favor.

Sometimes chalk cakes holds thicker than the pancake make-up hiding a transvestite's stubble. In these cases even a vigorous scrubbing with a toothbrush is ineffective. This is the time to get out a soft, copper-bristled brush (such as for cleaning kitchen pans). Apply very gentle pressure and work in a slow, circular motion to lift the chalk off the hold. Do not press hard or scrub fast or you could carve into the hold itself.

In agreement with the State Park officials, members of the El Paso Climber's Club wash off the holds at Hueco Tanks.

Limestone, volcanics, and most sandstones are particularly susceptible to overbrushing. Don't press any harder than if you were brushing your own teeth with the copper brush.

Certain holds, particularly very polished ones, can be easier to grip after they have been cleaned, then patted with fresh chalk. A thin residue of fresh, but not loose, chalk can impart a "grippier" texture. On very greasy holds, it sometimes pays to brush them clean, dab some fresh chalk on them to soak up any additional grease, then brush them clean again.

HOW TO MAKE FRIENDS & INFLUENCE BOULDERS & PEOPLE

Want to be the most popular boulderer at your home area? Get the permission of the area's owner or administrators, then give the chalk-choked boulders a good water wash. Chalk is water soluble; with enough water even the most caked problems will come clean. First, remove as much dry chalk as possible with standard brush and blow techniques. Then, if taps are available, spray with a hose. Otherwise, get a bug sprayer or a fire-fighter's water backpack pump unit to wash the holds. You may need to brush the holds while spraying them to get all the chalk off. This job is obviously easier if you have the help of several other boulderers or the local climbing club.

Warning #1 If you use too little water you will end up with drippy white stains descending from all the holds. You will have created an ugly mess.

Warning #2 In areas with rock art (such as Hueco Tanks), don't wash holds where the run-off will run over artwork.

Warning #3 In many areas the rock becomes more friable when wet—plan your washing so there will be adequate time for the holds to dry to maximum strength before climbing resumes. For example: don't wash them off the day before the weekend rush or the big bouldering contest.

Warning #4 Most areas will benefit from this treatment, but some areas might not. Obtain the advice and approval of the locals before acting. They might know some reason why water washing might be detrimental.

HOLD DRYING

If you're dying to try a problem with wet holds but can't wait for it to dry naturally, there are several strategies depending on how wet the holds are. First off, however, determine if the rock type is one that becomes fragile when wet, such as soft sandstone or volcanic rock. If so, stay off the problem until it dries thoroughly on its own and the holds regain their maximum strength. This usually takes at least 24 hours. On certain rock types, like most granite or quartzite, this is not a problem. When in doubt as to the solidity of the rock, ask for local advice or err on the side of caution. Breaking a key hold off a classic problem is not something you want to live with.

Assuming a strong rock type, the first step is to sponge up as much moisture as you can with a towel, rag, T-shirt, etc. If there's a breeze (or if you fan the hold), the remaining moisture may then escape to the air in a minute or two. This is the ideal scenario, as it leaves the hold super-clean and chalk-free. If the hold remains moist, then dab some chalk on it to soak up the moisture. It's important to sponge off the hold first or you will end up with a pasty mess of wet chalk on the hold and a resulting prolonged clean-up. (When a hold is in this condition, you need to wipe and/or scrape the paste out, then repeatedly apply chalk and remove the paste until the paste becomes dry enough to brush off.) Even if you sponge the hold well, you will probably need to go through the chalking process several times to dry it completely.

ROSIN

Also known as pof (rhymes with hoof), rosin is popularly used at a few European areas, most notably the famed boulder fields of Fontainebleau, in France. It is a tacky drying agent used on hands and boots. It is wrapped into a fist-sized ball in a dishtowel or old T-shirt, forming what looks like a Halloween ghost decoration. It is not water soluble. Therefore it is very hard to clean off of the rock. Rosin users whack the rock with their pof rags to prepare the holds. Repeated applications of rosin eventually cover up the texture of the natural stone and impart a slick, greasy texture that is jingus to hang onto without more rosin. Starting to sound a lot like heroin, right? Because of its deleterious effects, rosin use has not been accepted at any bouldering area in America. If you see climbers using rosin in the U.S., kindly ask them to refrain. If they refuse, tell them where they can shove their pof ball. Better yet, do your boulders a favor and confiscate it.

CLEANING YOUR BOOTS

Clean boot soles stick better to holds than dirty soles. Pit a pair of clean $20 hand-me-downs against a pair of dirty $140 super slippers with the latest sticky rubber—the cheap clodhoppers will win every time. Sticky rubber loves to stick to dirt just as much as it does to rock.

For Good Performance

The easiest way to clean your soles is to wipe your feet on a clean carpet patch at the base of the problem on each attempt. Frequently beat the dirt out of your carpet to keep it clean—there's no use wiping your feet on a dirty rug. (This is why fixed rugs don't work—99 per cent of the time they are dirty

The toe of the boot on the left has been spit-shined, the boot on the right only wiped on a carpet patch.

pieces of trash. It's a safe bet that climbers who are too lazy to carry their own rugs are too lazy to maintain those they've left behind.) Also be sure the footholds are clean on the problem. There's no sense in cleaning your boots, only to dirty them on the first footholds.

If you forget your rug, you can use a sweatshirt or T-shirt, or wipe your feet on your trouser legs, socks (if you're wearing them), or across the suede leather uppers of your boots. To keep one foot clean while wiping the other this way, stand on your heel and keep your toes raised above the ground. This will get your heel dirty, but as one is usually climbing on his or her toes, this is seldom a concern.

For Better Performance

For increased performance on difficult problems it's worth washing the soles of your boots. I usually spit some clean saliva (no gooey, candy-striped hawkers, just the clear, watery stuff) into the palm of my hand and rub the toe of my boot until it is clean. You can also use water and a rag, or, if you're feeling really anal, rubbing alcohol. To start a spit-shine, I first pat the excess chalk off my hands. I may even spit-wash my hands first, so that when I work on my boots I will not be rubbing a chalk/saliva mixture onto them. When spit-shining your soles you will feel the friction of the rubber gradually increase. When the sole is clean it should make a squeaky sound when you rub it, and/or your hand will chatter across the sole instead of sliding across it. If you need the heel clean for a tough heelhook or the instep clean for a rand-smear, clean those areas too.

For Utmost Performance

For utmost performance on the most desperate of problems—those you'd give a tooth or testicle to make it up—it's time to scrape the old, oxidized rubber off the soles. Rubber, no matter how clean it is, sticks better if it is unoxidized. For this purpose I have a "boot stick" a cobbler made for me. It consists of a 1-½" by 6" chunk of thick boot rubber with one side covered by a patch cut from a coarse grinding belt. Often it is enough to just rub the rubber side against the boot sole. A small layer of rubber will rub off, sometimes looking like the debris from a pencil eraser. Be sure to brush this debris off. Left behind will be a fresh layer of clean rubber with that dark-black, "just out of the box" look. On stubborn boots, or for fast cleaning of large areas, the grinding belt side works best. If you don't have a boot stick, or forget yours, you can always rub two boots together and get the same results. If I try a problem with really dinky toe holds and I only need the tip of my shoe clean, I will rub the toe of my shoe across the rand of my other shoe until I see that fresh black color appear. I do this after I have wiped my feet off on my rug, but before I step onto the problem. Quite obviously, repeated rubbing or grinding of your soles will wear them out more quickly—there's a reason that cobbler gave me a boot stick. Unless you

Chris Raypole at Gloria's,
Flagstaff, Arizona.

have money to blow or get your shoes for free, I would use this method sparingly.

Often, when you wash your soles or rub/grind to a fresh rubber layer, you will be sitting somewhere other than at the base of the problem. Be careful not to get your freshly cleaned soles dirty when walking to the problem. Walk on your heels, keeping your toes out of the dirt. If it is muddy, make a path of stepping stones to the base, taking care to position them where you won't fall on them. Some boulderers put their feet into plastic grocery bags and walk to the problem, not taking the bags off until they step onto the rock. Others, who frequently climb in muddy areas, get a pair of over-sized galoshes for this purpose.

It is very easy to spend five minutes cleaning your boots, cautiously walk over to the problem, then, just as you step onto the rock, your toe rolls into the dirt as you push off the ground, negating all that time-consuming prep work. To prevent this common mishap, you can position a small, clean stick or stone under your toe while you are standing on your heels. When you take off, your toe will roll up onto the stick or stone and will not touch the dirt. (If you are ethically opposed to cheater stones, such as I am, you will want to make sure the stick or stone you do this with does not give you an unsporting reach advantage on the first move.) Do not fall into the trap of thinking that you can walk over to a carpet patch at the base of the problem, then let your toes down once they are on the carpet. Unless you bought the carpet brand-new that day and had never wiped your feet on it, it will contain enough dirt to reduce the efficacy of your cleaning job.

If your shoes become dirty during the course of a problem, say from a dirty or crumbling foothold, wipe them off on your opposite pant leg. If you are wearing shorts you can wipe across the upper of your other shoe (sometimes awkward or impossible), or, if it's not too sweaty, the inside of your calf. If you can't get in balance for these tricks, you can wipe your foot across a clean patch of rock to knock grit off or tap or kick the rock to dislodge grit. Sticky rubber, however, is tenacious, and these last two tricks don't always work.

HARD-TO-SEE HOLDS

Sometimes problems require blind reaches to out-of-sight holds. To dial in to such a hold, make a mental note of visible features in line with the hold: examples are distinctive lichen patches, a water streak, a hairline seam, a ripple in the stone, even the edge of a shadow (though the latter is obviously ephemeral). When reaching for the hold, follow the line of these natural markers. Sometimes the line might not follow any markers, but you might know to reach around the corner six inches above the dime-sized blob of moss. This takes practice to get good at, but proficiency in this skill generates beaucoup style points.

Many boulderers opt for the easy way out and just draw a

Some selfish, used-kitty-litter-for-brains cretin made a mess of this boulder with his tick marks, then left without cleaning them off.

chalk line pointing to the hold. This is called a tick mark. Unfortunately, this tactic has gotten out of hand at many areas, to the point that some climbers will draw tick marks toward every hold no matter how big it is, or whether it is visible or not. This reeks of amateurism and laziness and does nothing to improve one's technique, especially for on-sighting. No wonder tick marks are also called "rookie stripes." Moreover, it creates a mess. Whereas chalked holds are often mistaken by nonclimbers to be some kind of water stain, natural precipitate, or guano blotch, tick marks are obviously unnatural and amount to little more than climbers' graffiti. Viewed as graffiti, tick marks quickly become a threat to access. No access, no bouldering, you don't get better. If you see tick marks, brush or wash them off. Leftover tick marks make climbers look bad and take the fun out of problem solving.

When I see climbers smear chalk on footholds to mark them, I wonder if their moms drank a lot when they were pregnant. These climbers might as well have wiped dirt on their shoes before they stepped on the problem. Chalk sticks to rubber just like dirt does, and reduces the rubber's stickiness. Of course, if a problem is too easy for you, you might try this trick to make it harder.

If you can't find any natural markers and you can't dial into a hold without help, have a partner point to it with a hand, an extendobrush, a stick, or a shadow. Hell, if it's dark, have him or her use a flashlight. If none of this works and you feel you must mark a hold, do so with a faint thumbprint. (With footholds, put the fingerprint next to them, not on them.) Your eye will be drawn to the hold just as well and you will have an easier time brushing it off when your session is over.

CHEATER STONES

Cheater stones are objects, usually rocks, stacked underneath a problem so climbers can reach holds they couldn't reach by standing on the ground. I believe that getting to the first holds is a part of every problem and I strongly disapprove of using cheater stones for this purpose. To be more blunt, for me to give advice on how to use them would be like the Pope giving advice on using condoms. Still, in the interest of completeness, objectivity, and curbing overpopulation, I will strike a deal. I will tell you what I know about their use, if John Paul II will preach some birth control. I'll go first.

- By placing a cheater stone at the base of a route, a climber instantly creates a bad landing. Falls onto cheater stones have sprained or broken more than a few ankles. If possible, have a partner remove the stone the instant you pull onto the rock or kick it away yourself. Take care not to fall on your partner. Some cheater stones will be too big to move quickly enough and are best left in place so the climber knows where the danger zone is.

Dave Lanman avoids his cheater stone after trying his luck on a Gill lunge at the Gunks, New York.

- Climbers will often stack several rocks to gain the height they desire. Take the time to make a stable stack. Toppling off a shifting cheater stone before getting on the rock is a quick path to embarrassment and rolled ankles. Occasionally a climber will start off an unstable stone to make it easier to kick it away as soon as he or she steps off it.
- Remove cheater stones after your attempt.
- Remember the words attributed to Britain's legendary Joe Brown (5'4"). When asked how he reached the first holds on some notoriously reachy gritstone problems, Brown responded, "I climb up to them."

If you can't reach the first holds, there is no rule that says you can't jump off the ground to get to them. Some fabulous problems, such as Hueco Tanks' *That's My Daughter* (aka *Jump Start*), begin this way.

Taking the idea behind cheater stones a step further, some boulderers have used ladders to partially ascend a wall before they start climbing. Instead of trying to avoid the first moves completely, this is done to facilitate working on moves higher on the problem by not expending energy climbing up to them. I dislike this idea even more than cheater stones. For me to advise on the use of ladders would be like the Pope endorsing abortion. I'll just say I wouldn't want to fall on one and if you use one you risk having your soul rot in hell.

Okay, I'm done talking about this. John Paul, it's your turn.

POWER SPOTS

I tell you it feels like I'm typing on this keyboard with bamboo shoots driven under my fingernails. Every keystroke I expend discussing power spotting is agonizing. Nevertheless, it's your honor at stake if you choose to use this tactic, so in the interest of completeness here goes.

Power spotting is the practice of having a spotter push a climber up or along a problem, taking a portion of that climber's weight so the climber can rehearse moves he or she can't do otherwise. This process is then repeated with the spotter taking less and less weight off the climber, until eventually the climber does the problem without the spotter's assistance.

Proponents of power spotting say it allows one to get stronger and do any given problem quicker. Personally, I'd rather spend that same time climbing problems I can do on my own and getting stronger and better that way. I'll gain more experience by climbing more problems and I'll have more fun. When I'm ready to go back to the original problem I couldn't do before, I'll have that many more ticks under my belt and the confidence that comes with that.

Power spots, cheater stones, and tick marks are gambits to bring a problem down to one's own level. I recommend eschewing these tricks and bringing one's abilities in line with the true difficulty of the problem. The extra strength and technique gained working a problem in the latter style will benefit you on all subsequent problems. As always, the reward received is proportionate to the effort expended.

Chris Eklund on "Mike's Left," Taylors
Falls, Wisconsin.

The Mental Game

Unlike the physical aspects of bouldering, there are no sure-fire regimens to develop your mental strength. Ninety per cent of bouldering is mental, yet most climbers spend ninety percent of their time trying to get their muscles strong. If that time were spent training one's brain, one would be much better off. When used to capacity, the mind becomes a Saturn booster, ready to lift you to new heights. When allowed to languish, the mind becomes a big fat sea anchor, holding you back until you reel it in. Yogis levitate. Why not you?

THINK POSITIVE

Feed on previous successes. Success isn't dependent upon reaching the top of a problem. I did zero problems when I bouldered two days ago. It was a successful outing because I had fun and learned from my mistakes. Next time out I will improve upon my last performance.

Some people psych up better by adopting a "I might as well try it even though I can't do it attitude." Whether you prefer a positive or negative mind set, I suggest telling yourself to try your hardest each time you touch the rock.

BREAK PROJECTS INTO REACHABLE GOALS

If a problem is taking you several tries, days, or even weeks to figure out, then set a goal each time out to make it an inch further up, or figure out a better way do a certain move. Every time you learn something, you become a better boulderer. I recall being psyched to flapper a fingertip when working on the Upper Meathook at Horsetooth Reservoir. My goal for that day was to put more weight on the tiny hold I was dynoing for than the last time out. That flapper was proof of progress. The next time out I set the goal to stall on that hold before falling.

PREVISUALIZE

Climb the problem in your head before you get on the rock. Run through all the moves, not just the crux. Think in real time, feeling every weight switch, every sharp hold, each muscle stretching and contracting. Don't forget the footwork. Think of how you will feel standing on top.

Mike Paul on "Big Bob's Big Wedge," Joshua Tree, California.

RELAX

Don't waste energy prior to getting on the rock. Save all your energy for doing the moves. Let your mind tell your muscles to relax. Run through a mental checklist of body parts from toes to head. Do they all feel loose? Are you tensing any muscles in anticipation of the problem? Focus on relaxing the tense muscles. Feel the tension drain from your body at the base of the boulder. Breathe deeply through your nose, then feel your body loosen as you exhale through your mouth. Relaxing is both a mental and physical technique. Practice it at home and at work so it becomes second nature when you step up to your next challenge.

AVOID SHORTCUTS

Avoid shortcuts like not cleaning shoes before warm-up problems. Clean them every time. Every bit of energy you waste adds up. Do things right and success will follow.

CAN THE EXCUSES

Don't blame your failures on gear or physical weakness. Unless you recently lost a limb or you're wearing rollerblades instead of rock boots, these are lame excuses. Look for the real cause. Do you need to improve your technique? Concentrate more? Readjust your goals?

WHOSE PROBLEM IS IT?

Think of how you will do a problem, not how someone else does it. Time spent worrying about how somebody else is climbing is time wasted. If you spent that time evaluating your own climbing and how to improve it, you would end up far ahead of the pack. Learn to recognize your weaknesses, then train them.

BE HONEST WITH YOURSELF

There can only be one best boulderer in the world. I personally know that she's a Nubian grandmother who fires V17 in bare feet to get grain from a storage hut located atop a boulder in the sweltering Sudanese desert. So where does that leave the rest of us? Free to become the best we can be. If you concentrate on that goal, then everything else—fame, fortune, inner peace, bad skin—will take care of itself. A good way to focus on this goal is to climb problems you want to do, not those that others want you to do.

Ego On The Rampage Part 500:
The Most Famous Boulder Problem in the World.

Due to its difficulty, aesthetics, and position smack dab in Yosemite's notorious Camp 4, Midnight Lightning *has become the most famous boulder problem in the world. Time and again climbers would accost me and say, "You're such a big boulderer. Have you ever done* Midnight Lightning?" *I could have replied, "No, but I've done scores of harder problems," but I knew this answer wouldn't cut it. Never mind that neither Gill, Holloway, or Murray had ever sent it, in many climbers' eyes, climbing* Midnight Lightning *was tantamount to a baptism into the boulderers' Hall Of Fame. Rather than try to convince them otherwise, I felt obliged to make the pilgrimage and come to grips with this "problem of problems." At the end of a very successful winter at Hueco Tanks, I was feeling strong and ready. I was also feeling a lot of pressure to prove myself. I put the rest of my life on hold and drove to Yosemite.*

Whenever anyone steps up to Midnight Lightning *a crowd of spectators thickens around the base like iron filings drawn to a magnet.*

*"Bachar Cracker,"
Camp 4, Yosemite,
California.*

Stories abounded of locals chasing wannabes away from the problem so that they wouldn't grease up the holds for the "real climbers." It was as if each successful ascent of this testpiece served to diminish its formidable reputation. I felt like a boxer entering the ring intent on taking away the hometown champ's title belt. I thought the crowd wanted to see me fail. In retrospect, I'm sure that most of this negative energy was of my own making. Doubtless, most of the crowd wanted to see somebody pull off the testpiece.

Utilizing my strength and maximizing my reach, I made it to the lip several times with no great difficulty. Getting over the lip was another story. My lanky limbs felt ill-suited for a straight mantel, so I tried planting my right foot on the lip and laying away with my left fingers placed high on a terribly sloping bump. I climbed up to this position a few times before I felt comfortable letting go of the right hand undercling at the lip and committing to the move. I was pushing the move out. With every inch my body rose, the layaway bump felt greasier and greasier. My face was plastered against the wall so I couldn't see the finishing thank-god hold. My right arm was waving above me searching for that hold. I asked the crowd, "How far?" but heard no reply. I took the silence to mean I was still a foot away. Should my left hand pop, I would take a sideways fall and risk breaking my wrist like a friend had on this same move. Worse yet, I might land on my head. I jumped. I missed my sketchpad by several feet and felt a pain like a nail being driven into my heel. I sucked up the impact with my legs, until my knee hit my chin and drove a canine tooth through my lip, nearly puncturing through both sides.

Compounding my anguish was the news that I had been just a few inches shy of the finishing hold. If the crowd had come looking for blood, they got it. I couldn't have fallen from any higher up. Knowing that, I felt success was only a try away. I could stand on my toes, but certainly not on my heel. Since I wouldn't be weighting that heel while trying the problem I hopped on one foot to the base. The pain drove some sense into me. I decided to go to the medical clinic and have my foot X-rayed. If it were only bruised, I would try the problem again that afternoon. That way I would have plenty of rest.

As it turned out, my heel was fractured. After a long, miserable drive back to El Paso, I crutched out of my car to an unenthusiastic embrace from my soon to be ex-girlfriend. She couldn't have cared less whether I had climbed it or not. I had been so obsessed with bouldering that I had been ignoring her.

A year later I drove back to Yosemite. I took a set of crutches with me, just in case. Camp 4 was closed, so no crowd flocked to watch. This was fortunate, because even though I was too scared to commit to the lip moves without a spot, I came to appreciate the problem for its beautiful moves and aesthetic line. I no longer wanted to climb Midnight Lightning to impress others, I just wanted to climb it.

Shortly thereafter, I returned with a spotter. A small crowd formed but was not distracting like before. This time I bounced several sticks off the wall above the lip and positioned my sketchpad where they landed. After a half-dozen sorties to the lip, I abandoned my previous sequence, made harder by a broken hold. I still had enough gas to get to the lip. For want of any better strategy, I opted to try the mantel I had previously regarded as applicable only to short climbers. Halfway through my first mantel attempt, I felt a strange weight shift as my left palm lifted slightly from the sloping mantel shelf. My weight became distributed between my right foot on the lip and my left forearm which was pressing against a steep flared groove/ramp. My arm greased out and I went flying. This time I landed unscathed, save for a juicy raspberry on my forearm.

Success seemed imminent. I chalked my forearm up and climbed to the lip once more. To get to this point I had put in a lot of work: I'd waited until I was strong enough, and called on years of experience. I'd cleaned all hand- and footholds meticulously between attempts and carefully primed my boots. I had waited patiently for cool temperatures. I had previsualized all the moves and ran them through my head as I relaxed before each attempt. I'd utilized tricks like the stick toss and chalking my forearm. I did everything right, but for the wrong reasons. Perhaps that's why I got slapped down on my initial attempts. This time though, my motives were purer. I felt no negative energy tugging down on me at the lip. All I felt was my weight shift from my palm to my forearm, and then to the fingers of my right hand as they curled onto to the final hold. A few minutes later I was back at my van. I reached into the cooler and pulled out a special bottle of beer on which I had drawn a lightning bolt.

The bitter beverage tasted oh so sweet.

Cocaine Corner,
Camp 4, Yosemite,
California.

When climbing problems like "Deep Six
Holiday" on Colorado's Independence
Pass, a single mistake could end a
career—good strategy is a must.

CHAPTER 7

Strategy and Avoiding Mistakes

Most of us have had the experience of being burned off on the boulders by physically weaker individuals. Their technique seemed no better than ours, and damned if they weren't wearing the same shoes we were. We wanted the problem even worse than them, so what's the deal? Why did they succeed where we floundered? Because they used good strategy and they didn't make mistakes.

BOULDERING STRATEGY

Bouldering strategy consists of decisions made before you get on a problem, or between attempts. Good strategy should be used on all problems, not just ones that trouble you.

- First off, find the descent. There's nothing quite so embarrassing to a boulderer as styling some problem to the top of a boulder, only to find out he or she can't get back down. Walk around the boulder first to find the easiest way down. If it looks tricky, it might pay to climb up first to familiarize oneself with the moves.
- Stand back from the problem and scope it from a distance. What look like great holds from the base of a problem often reveal themselves to be sloping butter dishes when you get a true perspective. This is especially important if you plan to dyno to a specific hold. You may also discover that a key hold is dirty.
- Check the topout from above. Is there a hidden hold? Are the final moves dirty? Covered in wet leaves? Will you bonk your head on a tree branch when you step up on the lip?
- Previsualize a sequence. Look at the problem and imagine yourself doing it. Where will your hands go? Where will your feet go? Which way will your body shift? Where will you land if you fall? Feel yourself doing the moves. Feel how your weight shifts; how that sideways move will twist your fingers on that knob. Climb the entire problem in your head before you grab the first holds.

Chris Jones checks out the exit moves on a high-ball problem before attempting it.

- Previsualize an alternate sequence before you attempt the problem. Suppose you climb halfway up a problem and find that your initial previsualized sequence doesn't work. You can either downclimb or jump off, or you can make use of your ascent to that point and try your alternate sequence. In this way, you don't burn up extra gas getting to the same spot a second time to try a different sequence.
- Anticipate your fall angles and discuss them with your spotter. Tell your spotter how you plan to try the problem and at which angles and on which moves you think you might fall. After this step, forget about falling and concentrate on succeeding.
- Put everything in your favor. Clean handholds and footholds. Clean your boots. If you won't be chalking up en route, leave your bag on the ground. Make sure the sun won't be in your eyes.
- Develop a psyching-up routine. This can be anything from peaceful meditation to kicking a punching bag, from screaming at your partner to whispering to the boulder. Find what works for you. My routine goes like this: I think of similar problems I have done. I think of how smoothly I will do the moves. I think of how it will feel when I latch on to the crux crimper. I remember that feeling from other problems. I give that feeling a one-syllable name: I call it "stick." I think of the crux move and I think "stick." I imagine how good I will feel pulling over the top. While I'm doing all this I am relaxing my muscles. I feel my arms get heavy as they relax. I feel them pull down on my shoulders and gently stretch my neck muscles. By this time I have dumped all extraneous thoughts. By doing so I feel light and focused. I concentrate on the moves as I rub chalk into my fingers. I run through my previsualized sequence one more time, thinking "stick" on the hard moves and a lip-stretching grin on the summit. Finally, if it's really hard, I'll spit just before I step on the problem. That extra five grams might hold me back, you know.

Dean Potter resting between attempts.

- Rest long enough between attempts. The tendency to jump right back on a problem after you pop off is great, but your chances of success increase if you rest until you feel like new. Give a buddy a spot, clean the holds on your problem, spit shine your boots, do some relaxation exercises…anything to give your body adequate rest before the next attempt.
- Don't get stuck on bad beta. If your sequence isn't working, try something new. Rule out moves that won't work: for example, a reach you can't make or a knee bar you won't fit.

- If you are getting tired and falling off a move you've already done, it's time to get off of that move. You may think you're getting stronger by working your muscles to exhaustion, but at the same time you are training your muscles to fail on that move. Even if you go back fresh, your muscles will say, "We don't have to contract as far to do this move," and you'll come up short again. "Practice makes permanent;" so says Bob Williams, the famous late '60s/early '70s boulderer. It's a bitch trying to erase bad muscle memory.
- When too tired to work on the crux moves, work on the finishing moves. Get them wired while you're tired so they won't feel foreign when you finally do climb through the crux to them.

In short, use your mind to save your body.

True Combat Story #88—The Real Victory

I don't care if you're John Gill, Jerry Moffat, or Fred Nicole—if you're a devoted boulderer it's likely that your list of desperate problems you couldn't do is nearly as long as the list of desperates you did crank. The Brits call V0, V-naught. I jokingly rate any problem I can't do as V-not. Most of my V-nots were problems I'd give up on after a few days, planning to return to them when I was ready. When it came down to it, I would have rather been climbing something I could do than flailing on something I couldn't. Nevertheless, I wanted one problem at Hueco Tanks so bad that I returned day after day. It was a beautiful sit-down start to Lip Service. I dubbed it Full Service.

Feeling territorial and insecure, I asked other climbers to stay off my prize. Some were stronger than me, and I was afraid they'd bogart

Diane French at Ilium Boulders, near Telluride, Colorado.

the sequence I'd worked so hard to discover. Days stretched into weeks, winter gave way to spring, and still I could not link the first two moves with the rest of the problem. I was so obsessed that I would wake in the wee hours and watch the sun rise as I drove into the park. I would have an hour to try the problem before it got too hot. Every time out I felt sure I'd crank it. Every time I'd gag on the same micro-toe hook.

I returned next season with Full Service at the top of my list. By this time, the mental block was firmly in place. Every time I tried to link it, I'd yank my toe off. It was as if I needed this problem to fail on, to teach me some kind of lesson. I was plenty strong enough, but I'd tuned my muscle memory to fail on this one move. My frustration built, as did my conviction that I'd found the only sequence that would work. Hence, I didn't try new sequences. I was climbing stupidly in more ways than one. Bob Williams watched me fail time and again. He watched me practice failing. He warned me that "practice makes permanent," and he was right. He also bluntly added that being first to do a route is no big deal if nobody else is trying it. Harsh, but true.

I started to hear rumors that someone else had climbed it and was staying mum so as not to blow my buzz. I wondered whether those rumors were true or made up to blow my buzz. Maybe both. I was ripped to the gills and down to 161 pounds, my lightest in ten years. Nevertheless, I had a ton of garbage in my head.

Later that season Dale Goddard climbed it, claimed it, and renamed it Serves You Right. The name was pointed, but appropriate. Had I respected others' rights to try it too, perhaps they would have respected my desire to bag it first. What's more, Dale had found a much easier sequence. My own stupidity had cost me the first. Had I not been so pigheaded, I might have discovered that sequence or the even easier moves discovered later.

Though I didn't climb it, I learned more from Full Service than from any other problem. Perhaps that mental block existed for my own benefit. Perhaps it remains there for the same reason. Had I bagged the first, I might not have learned the fruitlessness of territoriality, the "Practice makes permanent" principle, and the ugliness of disrespect. Dozens of boulderers have climbed Full Service now. I doubt anybody gained as much from it as I did.

Moral: The only failure is an experience from which you fail to learn.

AVOIDING COMMON MISTAKES

- *Don't just grab the top of a problem and then jump off.* Go ahead and push out the mantels. Manteling may be out of vogue these days, but it works the triceps as few climbing moves do. Building up your antagonist muscles can help prevent tendon and joint injuries. It's no surprise that so many climbers have such injuries because they spend all day pulling and no time pushing.
- *Don't be afraid to learn from "less experienced" climbers.* The second you think you know it all is the second you cease to learn and improve. I've learned plenty from old sages, but I've also picked up a lot from young punks who were in diapers when I cranked my first B1s.
- *Don't fall victim to the ratings game.* Time spent worrying about ratings is time wasted. Climb problems for their beauty, not for their numbers. Would you rather have someone call you by your name or a number?
- *Don't rely on the sequences of others.* Unless that other climber is your identical twin, chances are your body is better suited to a different sequence. Go ahead and experiment.
- *Don't be afraid to fall.* Falling is not failing. It is an integral part of the bouldering game (unless you're high bouldering or cranking above a bad landing). If you aren't falling, you aren't pushing yourself. If you don't push yourself, you won't improve.
- *Don't forget about the footholds.* A common mistake made when previsualizing is to concentrate on the hand sequence and forget about your feet. All of a sudden the climber has to ad lib, making up a sequence as he or she goes. This takes time and wastes energy.

Don't just grab the top of a problem and then jump off. Mark Wilford presses out the mantel on "Pinch Overhang," Horsetooth Reservoir.

two concussions, stitches

tendon & ligament
damage in four fingers

bad '80s haircut

tendinitis

tendinitis

degenerative
back pain,
scarification

torn tendon

broken wrist

aggravated
arthritis
in both hips

tendon & ligament
damage in four more fingers

bone-deep
shin lacerations

tendinitis behind
both knees

fractured heel

bunion city

broken
sesmoid

In between injuries the author
celebrates after flashing "The Ripper
Traverse," Pueblo, Colorado.

Health and Injuries

Despite its reputation as being relatively risk-free, bouldering should not be taken lightly. Most boulderers do many more hard moves in a day than they would if they were roped climbing. Moreover, every bouldering fall is a ground fall. These two attributes alone greatly increase the chances of injury. Quite a few climbers claim that their worst injuries have resulted from bouldering. This chapter will discuss the most common bouldering injuries and how to prevent them.

ANKLES AND WRISTS

Other than bruised egos, sprained ankles and wrists are the most common bouldering injuries. You will note that my personal injury list does not include any ankle sprains. How did I pull this off after over 20 years of bouldering? By doing my ABCs. I once sprained my ankle descending from a roped climb and the doctor gave me ankle exercises to restrengthen that joint. Basically, they consist of holding your leg out or supporting it so the foot hangs freely, then tracing the alphabet in the air with your foot. Make believe you have a crayon between your toes and write letters as big as possible to work as great a range of motion. Move your foot, but keep your leg still. The only joint motion should be in your ankle and the letters will be about a foot high. You should feel some ankle stretching while you do this, and after running through the alphabet once or twice your shins will be burning. You can do these exercises watching TV; on the bus to school; behind a desk at work; or if you have trouble remembering batting averages, in bed while having sex. I've done my ABCs every day for 11 years and now my ankles are wickedly strong. I've taken many falls in that time where my ankle rolled viciously, but every time I felt fine a day or two later. Start writing now before you read the next paragraph.

Some people believe in stretching their ankles out. My doctor says to go easy on this, as some tightness in the ligaments is necessary to hold the joint together.

The same advice applies for wrists as well: strengthen them in all directions and don't over-stretch them.

Though the author is strengthening his ankle through its full range of motion, he displays poor style by blocking his view of the TV.

Different styles of taping to support tendons.

TENDONS

Tendon injuries are common amongst boulderers. They come in two basic types—overuse injuries and catastrophic injuries.

Overuse causes tendonitis that can be very painful and hard to get rid of. The best cure is rest. Don't do anything that makes it hurt more. Icing after exercise and popping ibuprofen can help with the pain and reduce the swelling. By reducing swelling, further irritation of the tendon is reduced. One must be wary, however, of painkillers. By masking the pain, they lure a climber into thinking he or she is healthy. As a result, the climber pushes hard on the rock again and only makes things worse. Rest until the pain vanishes, then work back slowly. Don't rush things. If you do you may be in for cortisone shots, ultrasound, joint casts, or even surgery. All that money you spend on your doctor could be spent on a trip to Fontainebleau. Of course, if your doctor is a climber too, that money might still go toward a Fontainebleau trip—be sure he sends you a postcard.

Catastrophic injuries range from minor tendon pulley tears to complete detachment of the tendon from the bone. The more scar tissue you have in your tendons (from overuse or previous pulls and tears), the more likely you are to suffer catastrophic injuries. John Gill had terrible bouts with elbow tendonitis when he was in grad school. It came back to haunt him decades later when, midway up a problem, his biceps tendon tore away from his elbow, causing his biceps to roll up like a window shade into his shoulder.

Many catastrophic injuries can't be avoided—they just happen. Many, though, can be dodged. Several times I have jumped from a problem after feeling a slight pulling sensation in my finger, palm, or wrist. I'd wonder if I had hurt something and if I should quit. I'd wait around for a few minutes, feel better, and tell myself: "I'll try the problem one more time. If it hurts again, I'll quit for the day." Almost every time I told myself this, I ended up quitting—not just for the day, but for months. I'd try the move that caused the initial stretching feeling, then I'd feel a terrible tearing sensation. One time it went from my fingertip to halfway up my forearm. It took six months to heal that time. Six months with no bouldering. If you think you might be injured but don't know for sure, play it safe and knock off for the day. If you can't do that, do some one-arm problems with your good hand. At the very least, try out your injured limb on an easy problem, not the one you just tweaked it on.

Taping Tendons

If you have had tendon or pulley tears in the past, it can pay to back up those scarred parts with tape. I tape rings around 10 to 12 different joints when I boulder these days. Sometimes I need to tape my wrists and elbows as well. This is because I didn't listen to my body when I was younger. I worry that the day will come when my friends finish bouldering before I'm done taping up.

SKELETON

Most people think of skeletal bouldering injuries as being just broken bones. If you screw up (and/or your spotter screws up), these are going to happen and there's not much you can do about it other than milk your friends for sympathy.

More insidious and more serious than broken bones is degeneration of the tissue between your bones, such as the disks in your spine. Multiple ground falls aren't good for you. Use a sketchpad whenever possible. Us old timers will do our best to make you feel soft and wimpy for doing this—after all, we cranked those problems without any of that sissy stuff and we're damn proud of it. Just look at us and say, "Wow! You guys were tough," then watch us limp away. Don't let us make you do something stupid. If I had it all to do over again (assuming we had the technology), I would use a sketchpad religiously.

MELON

If we used that appendage on top of our shoulders more, we probably wouldn't be climbers. Nonetheless, your melon (head) is worth protecting. Concussions and whiplash are both injuries suffered by boulderers. If you land on your head, you can expect a concussion. Prevention is easy: get a good spot and/or wear a helmet. Whiplash happens when someone hits the ground and his or her head snaps back without hitting anything. Again, a good spot is the answer.

This bouldering session was interrupted for several hours when I went to the emergency room to get a bone-deep gash in my scalp stiched.

Two-for-one Purple Heart Bouldering Stories

Two of my concussions came within five weeks of each other. Both times I was new to the area I was climbing in. Both times I felt I knew the rock better than I did. One time my hand slid off a sloper I thought was good. The other time my foot stuck in a groove I thought it would slip out of easily when I jumped. Both times it was on a warm-up problem at the beginning of the day. Both times I screwed up because I was taking things too casually. Don't underestimate the risks of bouldering.

FLAPPERS AND SKIN CARE

A flapper occurs when the rock gouges up a chunk of skin that remains partially attached to your finger or elsewhere. First we'll discuss how to treat an existing flapper, then we will talk about preventative skin maintenance.

If you've gouged up a choice divot and you want to continue bouldering, clean out the wound, then trim off any dangling

A juicy flapper.

leftover skin (the flapper itself) with your nail clippers. Okay, you've just clipped off the lid of the crater; now look around the walls. Is there any loose skin you can see under? Often there is. Many flappers are just the torn up lid of a thick blood blister. Slip the clippers under the edge of any loose skin (taking care not to irritate the sensitive raw patch at the base of the crater) and bevel the side of the crater. You don't want any loose overlapping skin left to initiate another possible snag. Tape over the crater and continue bouldering. Tufskin® or tincture of benzoin can be used to help the tape stick—and the latter gives you a burning sting to let you know you're still alive.

When a cut is on your fingertip and you don't want to wrap the whole tip in tape you can place a thin strip of tape just over the cut itself with Krazy Glue®. Put the glue on the skin, then press the tape on, taking care not to glue your fingers together.

If the gouge is really deep and you still want to continue bouldering, you can clean the wound and leave the flapper intact. Press it back into place or glue it down with Krazy Glue® (not Super Glue® which is toxic), then tape over it. The chunk of flapper will provide some extra padding for the wound. (Some people might find that Krazy Glue® irritates their skin. Use this technique sparingly.)

When you finish bouldering, pull the tape off, then trim off the dead skin and bevel the crater with your nail clippers (if you haven't already done so). You can further bevel and smooth the edges of the crater with an emery pad or board. Put an antibiotic ointment, such as Neosporin®, on the wound, then bandage it. Keep it covered. If you boulder within the next three days, tape over the wound while bouldering, then apply ointment and bandages afterwards. If treated right, on the fourth day the finger should be ready for climbing without tape.

To prevent flappers from occurring in the first place, remove all "pull tabs" (tiny flaps of peeling skin) from your fingers with the emery pad or nail clippers. Keep the surface of your fingers smooth, with no pull tabs or ridges to snag. Also, keep the skin moist and pliable. Those prized calluses you worked so hard to develop will last longer if they don't dry out. Furthermore, dry skin flappers easily. Pliable skin doesn't. To keep skin pliable, wash off chalk as soon as possible after each session. Use hand lotion after washing your hands. Before going to bed rub a little petroleum jelly on your fingers. This also helps prevent splitting. Keeping your skin soft may seem counterproductive to climbing. Some folks fear it may shorten the duration of their sessions. Session length, however, is a function of pain endurance, not skin toughness. Your nerves will adapt to long sessions and they, not your skin, will tell you when your fingers have had enough.

STRETCHING

When I started bouldering, Nat Smale ruled the local boulders. He cranked the problems the rest of us dreamed of doing. When Nat tried to touch his toes, his fingertips ended up a foot shy. He was that inflexible. I figured this was pretty cool, hence I neglected stretching for the early part of my career. Unfortunately, I never could do seven consecutive one-arm pull-ups like Nat. My lack of flexibility has haunted me ever since.

Unless you are so strong that you can climb everything without your feet, you need to stretch. Doing so before bouldering will help prevent injury. Doing so after bouldering will help increase flexibility. Particularly helpful are stretches to improve high stepping, hip turnout, and shoulder flexibility. Stretching the front and back of the forearms can help minimize tendinitis in the elbows. Check the library for books and articles on stretching.

John "Whitey" MacLean demonstrates the advantages of high step flexibility on "Try Again," Lincoln Woods, Rhode Island.

WARMING UP

Warming up is one of the most important steps to injury prevention. Get the muscles loose before hitting the hard problems. Do some calisthenics and stretching. Develop a circuit of easy problems that warms up each body part. You can combine some stretching while you do this by hanging on jugs, doing high steps, holding a wide stem, and so forth. Work up gradually through a few harder problems before jumping on your project.

RECOVERING FROM INJURIES

It took me about 18 years to learn how to recover from injuries. Before that I always struggled with the devastating psychological effects of not climbing. I now realize that an injury doesn't have to stop you from climbing; you just have to readjust your expectations. The best advice I received about dealing with climbing injuries was to go climbing. That's right: go climbing. The catch is you can climb, but you can't climb anything that makes the injury hurt. So if you hurt yourself on a 5.13, you might want to try a 5.4. If the 5.4 hurts, do a 5.2. If the 5.4 doesn't hurt, try a 5.5 next. If 5.4 sounds too boring, leave the rope at home, do it at night, climb it in a snowstorm, take a beginner out: heck, take your mom out. As I write this, I'm recovering from another bout of elbow tendonitis. I'm back up to 5.7 now. Sure, I wish I were cranking much harder, but at least I'm still climbing and I'm enjoying a bunch of climbs I might not have done otherwise.

A few days after severely bruising his foot in a bouldering fall, Eric Zschiesche maintains sanity by cranking problems one-footed at Blowing Rock.

Den Danna on "Instant Classic" at
Rumney, New Hampshire. By cleaning
only the necessary holds instead of
denuding a swath up the boulder, it only
took a few minutes to prepare this
problem for a first ascent. It received
second, third, and fourth ascents within
an hour of the FA.

First Ascents

Boldly going where no man or woman has gone before can be a thrilling experience. There is an extra adrenaline rush when you commit to a move with no idea of whether it will go or not. There's a sense of accomplishment and quite often the social perks that go along with that. There can be the reward of pitting yourself against a challenge set before you by nature, not by other climbers. Or, if competitive fires drive you, there can be the kick of picking a plum before your rival does. Whatever the reason one chooses to do a first ascent, one should put some thought into the project first.

HOW MUCH, IF ANY, TO CLEAN

Much of the responsibility involved in first ascents centers around the initial cleaning of the problem. There are ethical and environmental considerations. Usually the ethical considerations are tied closely to environmental factors. For instance, in some of the densely forested country of the southeast it may not raise any eyebrows if someone ripped 50 pounds of kudzu off a boulder to access a problem. On the other hand, I know of some Hueco locals who would gladly pummel anyone who removed a single leaf from one of the rare ferns in the park. In the south that kudzu might all grow back in a few months. In West Texas that fern might never recover. Before going at a boulder with your wire brushes, consider the effects it will have on the ecosystem.

Look at a problem objectively. (This is hard with first ascent stars twinkling in front of one's eyes.) Will it be a classic that others will want to repeat? Or an embarrassment that will dishonor you and your whole family? Doing a first ascent for the sake of doing a first ascent is the lamest reason I can think of. If the problem is not going to see much future traffic, perhaps it is best to clean it minimally or not at all. Maybe you'd be better off ignoring the problem altogether. Or you can climb it as nature presented it. Climbing on dirty holds is not impossible and actually good practice should you ever get hooked on mountaineering. (I reckon one reason top boulderer Mark Wilford is also such a great alpine climber is because he is not afraid to tackle a boulder problem without cleaning it. To him part of the challenge lies in effectively dealing with dirty holds while he climbs. After all, nobody was going to brush clean the North Face of the Eiger before he soloed it.)

Okay, you're convinced that people will wait in line and buy tickets to get on your proposed first. How to approach it then. Do you rip off every loose flake in sight, rent a grader to smooth out the landing, then call in the Air Force for an agent orange strike to devegetate it? This could be overkill. Once again, I suggest thinking objectively. How would the problem look if nobody cleaned it but a hundred people climbed it? All those ascents would rub the dirt and lichen off the hand- and footholds, snap off the loose flakes that people might actually pull on, leave the loose flakes that nobody pulled on, and so on. To avoid overcleaning, imagine what the climb would look like after that many ascents, then clean it to that point, but no further. You'll save yourself time (which you can spend on more problems) and you'll avoid excessive environmental damage (and maybe future access hassles).

An Alternative To First Ascent Mania:
Another Ego-Bloating First-Person Account

I have spent much of my bouldering career in the Southwestern United States. Time and again I would find an incredible virgin line to scale. Often I would succeed and come down grinning with the satisfaction of ticking another classic first ascent. We're talking another feather in the cap of the Great White Boulderer, explorer and developer of the finest problems in the land. More times than I care to remember, I would discover that Bob Murray had been up the problem before me. Well, pluck my cap like a Christmas goose. Usually this discovery would come months or years after my ascent. By that time, I was hot on some other first I had just done, so the disappointment was softened. Still, it became a recurring theme in my career. Strangely, it had a very positive effect. I grew to admire Murray's taste in problems immensely—after all, we were drawn to the same walls. More importantly, I realized that being first didn't mean that much—it was the sense of adventure that counted. When I was up on those problems I was jacked up on so much adrenaline that I'd shake uncontrollably as soon as I pulled over the top. Sometimes I had to wait several minutes to calm down enough to safely descend. It's great when several climbers can get a first ascent buzz from the same problem. For all we know, Bob may not have been the first up either.

In recent years I've done a number of fine probable firsts. In the spirit of multiple first ascents, I haven't shown others these routes. At one point, however, I suffered a lapse. Far out in a little-visited desert, I climbed a huge boulder with no easy route to the top. Confident that I was first to stand on top, I cockily stacked some tiny flakes into a two-inch tall cairn on the summit. I strongly doubt any other boulderer will ever find or climb that rock in the future, but if he or she does, I hope I will have returned first and swept that cairn off.

TOOLS OF THE TRADE

Diane French repeating a problem at the Mine Boulders, Telluride, Colorado.

Some boulderers make a career out of doing first ascents; others make a career without ever doing one. Sometimes, one may be fortunate enough to meet a virgin boulder problem that requires no hold cleaning. Usually, however, holds collect dirt, leaves, cactus spines, pine needles, and broken glass or are covered with varying amounts of moss, lichen, poison ivy, etc. Often, it can take longer to clean a problem than to actually climb it.

Wire brushes are the primary tool of the first ascensionist. A standard steel-bristled paint scrubbing brush (12-inch handle, 5 inches of bristles) found at any hardware store works well. In areas of soft rock, such as sandstone or limestone, steel-bristles can damage the rock, actually carving grooves if too vigorously applied. In these cases a brass-bristle brush, such as for scouring pots, is a better choice.

To clean thin cracks, tight corners, and pockets that the larger brush can't fit into, I use round plumber's brushes. These come in varying diameters and reside in the plumbing department at most hardware stores. Get the smallest (½-inch diameter) and a 1-inch too.

To clean holds you can't reach, make an extendobrush. Mine has the longest wooden mop handle I could find at the hardware store. A standard brush is pipe-clamped to one end, a plumbing brush to the other end. As well I have a skyhook bolted to the plumbing brush end. I use this to test loose flakes. The wire handle of the plumbing brush can be bent to angle in to hard-to-reach holds. If bent too frequently, the wire handle will fatigue and break.

On tall problems you may have to clean holds on the go. I once had a small wire brush on a string around my neck. This was uncomfortable and the bristles threatened to scrape off the chest hair I had worked so long to grow, so I was psyched when I learned of the gammon reel. This is a surveyor's gadget that has a retractable string going into a plastic case the size of a dental floss box. It's like those retractable key chains janitors wear, but very light. I wear the gammon reel on my chalk bag belt, and have a nylon brush and a wire brush on the string. I can reel out the brushes, clean a hold with the appropriate brush, then just drop the brushes and they snap back to my hip.

Safety glasses or goggles are helpful for keeping grit out of your eyes.

CLEANING TIPS

- Clean from the top down for the same reason you sweep stairs from the top down.
- On sloped holds and rounded bulges, clean not just the fingertip edge, but also the spots where your palm and/or forearm will rest against the rock. The extra friction on your palm or arm can be crucial to success.
- On holds that stick out like sore thumbs after they're cleaned, feather the edges of your cleaning job to blend in with the surrounding rock
- Don't overclean. This is a waste of time that could be better spent climbing. If you find that a problem needs more cleaning, you can always go back and clean it further.

EVALUATING LOOSE HOLDS ON VIRGIN LINES

You can save yourself injury if you test loose holds before you pull on them. When I can reach a hold from the ground I test it with my own fingers. Sometimes I will get a lot of flex and sense imminent breakage, yet the hold does not come off in my fingers, or I give up before I snap it into my face. Through much trial and error I came up with the following additional test: I stick the plastic handle of my toothbrush behind the suspect hold and twist. If the hold snaps, it most likely would have snapped if I pulled on it climbing. If the brush just flexes or snaps itself, the hold will probably support weight if treated correctly. (See the section on *Dealing With Loose Rock* in Chapter 2). Rarely would a hold fail that passed the toothbrush test. Testing with a stouter tool, say a screwdriver or cleaning pin, is overkill. After all, given a big enough crow bar, you could pry North America off the planet. To test holds out of reach, a skyhook attached to the end of a stick can be used. Pull on the holds in the directions you will pull on them while climbing. There's no sense in pulling off a hold by yanking on it at some oddball angle you wouldn't use while climbing.

Whatever method you use to test loose holds, remember that you usually won't have your entire weight on that hold. The hold might only need to support 30 pounds for you to do the move. If this is the case, don't test it to 180 pounds. If you do, your problem might end up shy one hold.

The Big Decision: Yet Another Blood-and-Guts Tale of Bouldering Action

Many years ago, I had the privilege to be turned on to an incredible boulder garden in the mountains. Very few people had been there, fewer still seem inclined to boulder there, yet there were literally dozens of killer boulders to develop. I was in boulderer's heaven. Here I could climb by my rules and develop an area as I saw fit. I got in a pattern of climbing one day, then cleaning problems the next day. As most of the boulders had never been climbed, there were a fair number of loose flakes adorning them. Some of these fell off with a brush of the hand, others with a gentle tug, and some withstood testing and remained to be used as holds. To test layaways out of my reach, I would take a shovel, put the corner of the blade behind the suspect flake, then, holding on to the end of the handle, I'd give a twist. (This may sound like overkill, but the actual torque you can exert this way is fairly low, probably not much more than with a toothbrush test.) I had climbed part way up one exquisitely beautiful problem, but had been spooked by the flexing layaway I would have to pull on—the only hold in an eight-foot span of rock. I gave it the shovel test: sure enough, it snapped off, but in such a way as to form a hold twice as big. The problem seemed substantially altered and I felt bad, like I'd doctored a hold instead of breaking a loose flake. I gave the resulting hold the same test, but it held fast. I told myself I wasn't a bad person and worked on the problem. It turned out to be so hard that I would never have stood a chance had the flake withstood its initial test.

A few days later in the same area I was testing a hold on another classic line. This hold also failed and dropped in the dirt at my feet. Like on the first problem, it was the only hold adorning a long blank stretch. Unlike the first problem, there was nothing left when it snapped off. The problem was gorgeous, a three-star candidate in any area. Now it wouldn't go for anyone less than eight feet tall. I knew with a little glue I could have that problem back. Carefully done and nobody but myself would know. Furthermore, there was a fair chance that I'd be the only person to ever try that problem; my choice would be entirely personal. Still, something didn't feel right about that tactic. At the base of the problem was a thick flake, half the size of a garage door. It leaned a few inches out from the wall. I placed the broken hold atop it and left to sleep on my decision.

A few days later I made up my mind. If I were to glue that hold back on, then by the same token, I should glue back all the holds I'd knocked off testing. To do otherwise would be to take nature's hand out of the decision. By removing the luck of the draw, I'd also remove much of the adventure of bouldering. I didn't want to be in the business of creating problems instead of cleaning them, so I walked over to the problem, picked up the broken hold, and dropped it down the narrow gap behind the starter flake. I would never be able to retrieve that hold, and I would never have doubt again about where I draw the line between cleaning and creation.

Chris Eklund repeating "Mike's Right,"
Taylors Falls, Wisconsin. The fixed rugs
need to be picked up and taken away.

GLUE

Glue is too often used as a substitute for technique. In the past I have felt that gluing a hold back on was sometimes justified when a hold snapped off of a classic problem. I felt others deserved to try that problem in the same state as the first ascensionist. Now I'm not so sure. Broken holds can be viewed as part of the evolution of a problem. Gill's famous *Right Eliminator* and *Standard Mental Block* problems (at Horsetooth Reservoir in Colorado) are examples of problems that have evolved substantially, hold-wise, through the years, but are still regarded as classics.

If one does resort to the glue pot to realize his or her ambitions, do the climbing community a favor: don't just drip glue around the edges of a hold to reinforce it. This causes a visual mess and is a weak fix. Instead, pull the hold off (you might find out you can't and therefore don't have to monkey with it), then clean off the back of the hold and the rock where it pulled off. Apply your glue to these surfaces and press the hold back on. You will have a much greater surface area to glue, hence a stronger bond. Also, the glue will be hidden behind the hold: all that will be visible is a hairline crack where the hold snapped off. Go easy on the glue as most glues used by climbers are space-filling epoxies. If you use too much, the hold will stick farther out, look stupid, and change the problem to boot.

There's a special place in Hell for people who turn the boulders into gluey messes. All the holds suck. Your chalk bag is empty. And your partner always botches the spot.

DOCTORING VERSUS CLEANING

Where does one draw the line between what constitutes cleaning a problem and what constitutes doctoring it? I believe the crucial factor is intent. If the preparation of the problem is done with an eye toward creating a problem of a certain difficulty, say four holds broke off when tested, and two were glued back on, then you most certainly are doctoring the route and you've brought shame upon yourself, your friends, your family, and your country. If you have chiseled in a new hold or filed down one that was too sharp for your piggies, then you too are a world-class loser. Using glue or a chisel to bring a problem down to your level permanently alters the problem, and everyone, not just you, has to live with your bungling. If nature doesn't provide the challenge you're looking for (or too much of a challenge for you), then go to the climbing gym to create your own routes.

Russ Bobzein buildering at the
UC Berkeley campus.

More Bouldering Games

BOULDERING IN THE COLD

Cold conditions can be great for bouldering. Your hands don't sweat, boots often stick better, and the crowds vanish. On the minus side, your fingers can get numb, your body is more prone to injury, and all those clothes hide your finely chiseled physique. A good warm-up is your best defense against injury. It also helps warm up the fingers. When fingers get numb during a problem you've got a real problem. Sometimes dipping into a warm chalk bag can help, if only to get them out of the wind. I've heard of climbers putting handwarmers in their chalk bags, though I haven't tried this myself.

BOULDERING IN THE RAIN OR SNOW

One of the best bouldering sessions I've had in recent years was at the Sugarloaf Boulder in Banff, Canada. Snow covered the boulder and it took us multiple attempts just to scale the third-class walk-off. By the end of the session, we were climbing problems we couldn't step off the ground on an hour before. We learned how to freeze our gloves to slopers, create holds with packed snow, brush snow off without smearing it, and so forth. For all I know, the hardest problem we did might have been 5.2, but it sure as hell didn't matter. We were having a blast and the glove-freezing trick came in handy for me years later on the Eiger. Bad conditions don't equate to bad bouldering. Use the opportunity to learn something. Practice having fun.

ICE BOULDERING

All the fun of rock bouldering with ten times the risk. Bouldering in crampons and drytooling with axes is great practice for mixed climbing. But just as it is foolhardy and dangerous to fall ice climbing, so it is equally foolhardy to fall bouldering with all those knives strapped to you. Toproping is probably a better choice. Nevertheless, some climbers do boulder on rock with their ice tools. If you do this, it is best to stay off established boulder problems and practice somewhere obscure. Crampons leave permanent scrape marks and drytooling puts incredibly concentrated stress on holds

Michelle Hurni and Rod Willard bouldering in their home gym.

with high potential for breaking them. Bouldering on ice is good practice too, and doesn't suffer from these drawbacks. Beware of tools popping off holds or out of the ice—they have a habit of heading straight for your face. Pad or remove your adzes when not in use and wear a helmet and eye protection.

AID BOULDERING

No, I'm not talking about power spots. Many a climber has learned direct aid techniques on the boulders before heading for the big walls. As a result, ugly old pin scars festoon many boulders. This is the '90s, and clean aid techniques have proved to be faster and less destructive than pitoning. Boulders can be a good place to learn hooking and nutcraft. As with dry tool bouldering, it is best to practice on an obscure boulder—stay off established free climbing problems. Hooks place tremendous strain on the holds that support them. A hold that supports a 200-pound boulderer by the fingertips of one hand may snap when hooked by a 110-pound climber. Like ice tools, when hooks or nuts pop they seem to ignore the laws of physics and head straight for your face. Wear a helmet and eye protection. Aid falls are sudden and often unexpected, making for rougher landings. Again, toproping is a good answer if you want to push your limits safely.

BUILDERING

Buildering is bouldering on buildings. Buildings often have far fewer surface flaws than boulders. This stark geometry forces precise technique. Buildering can be great practice and great fun. For some, it is an end unto itself. The liability is that it is quite often illegal.

PUMPING PLASTIC

I love being outdoors and I dig the feel of stone under my fingertips, the way it conducts heat and how every single hold is unique. Fortunately for me, the nearest boulders are just a few minutes' walk out my back door. Not all of us are so lucky, hence climbing indoors at commercial gyms or on home walls has become increasingly popular. For some people it is a good way to train for strength and technique, others enjoy it as an end in its own right. Certainly, it is the best place to train for competitions on plastic.

Because the holds can be moved about, you can create whatever climb you want, given the parameters of the wall you are bolting the holds to. You can do this to work very specific techniques. Certain techniques—drop knee comes to mind—are more easily learned on artificial walls, because of the abundance of large, protruding footholds. Some climbers build replicas of crux sections of routes found on real rock. Most bouldering games played outdoors can be played indoors as well. For liability reasons, commercial gyms might not let you set your own routes.

The biggest advantage of pumping plastic is its convenience—if it's raining or dark or a bunch of drunks are shooting bottles at the local boulders you don't have to go out in those conditions, you can get your fix indoors. Inside, the landings are usually cushy and conditions predictable. The disadvantage is that commercial gyms charge you to climb, and home walls are initially expensive and labor-intensive to build. Also, because a hold must be big enough to accept a bolt, it usually represents a large foothold, thus there are few opportunities to practice fine edging skills. This may change in the future with advances in hold design. Few gyms seem inclined to offer artificial slabs to practice footwork or cracks for jamming.

Training

In 22 years of climbing I have devoted maybe 6 months total to gym training. Training indoors bores me and I'd much rather spend my time climbing. I strongly believe that bouldering is the best training for bouldering. Hence, I've chosen to live my life where there will always be boulders nearby.

Bob Murray on the Streambed Traverse, Socorro, New Mexico.

TRAINING ON BOULDERS

Bouldering a lot will increase your strength. To build endurance, do long traverses or laps on shorter traverses. For building power, try doing moves static that you usually dyno. Try downclimbing problems statically. Try skipping past intermediate holds you would usually use. Make up a circuit of your favorite power problems and do laps on it. Better yet, spend the winter at Hueco Tanks and return home buff—like Arnold.

To better your footwork, do slab problems. Play around on the smallest holds you can find. Try climbing without your hands—this is great for your balance. On steeper problems, concentrate on doing them with as little weight on your hands as possible. Try them in ski gloves. You can work on your footwork when warming up or at the end of a session when your arms or tips are blown.

TRAINING IN THE GYM

I do feel that some basic weight lifting, especially with the antagonist muscles, could have spared me several injuries during my career. Unfortunately, I don't have a degree in exercise physiology so I don't feel qualified to dish out any gym training advice other than to say that there are plenty of books on the subject. If you can't make it out to the boulders 200 days a year, or if you're the kind of twisto who likes the gym, then head to the library to pump some pages. Good luck.

*John Gill at the Hagermeister Boulders,
Colorado.*

Photo: John Gill collection

Paths to Success

There is no single sure-fire path to bouldering success. The right path for you is the one that gives you the greatest satisfaction. The right path will depend on your temperament as much as your physique and ability. Following are quick sketches of the paths taken by some notable American boulderers.

JOHN GILL—THE GENIUS

The originator of modern bouldering strayed far from the path other climbers took at the time. He eschewed "three points on at all times" technique and started dynoing for holds on purpose. Unheard of. Furthermore, he directed his immense climbing talent toward bouldering as an end—not just as training for roped climbing. Hence, many of his fellow climbers regarded him as a kook. Now he is seen as a genius and somewhat as a Zen master of bouldering.

Gill applied not just gymnastic technique and strength to the boulders, but also a gymnastic mindset. To Gill, form was just as important as difficulty—a good gymnastic routine depended on both. Gill would repeat his problems over and over until he flowed across the rock, gaining maximum kinesthetic awareness. He didn't climb for the limelight or to compete with others. He climbed for the love of movement. Had he focused more on difficulty, his problems would have been that much harder. Anyone who has attempted to repeat his training tricks, like the one-armed front lever, can attest to that.

Gill put up hundreds of problems throughout the country. By virtue of their difficulty and history, Gill problems have become the most sought-after testpieces in American bouldering.

BOB WILLIAMS—THE COMPETITOR

Bob Williams loves to compete with others. It's where he gets his drive. As long as he is winning he is psyched. This made him one of the great boulderers of the late '60s and early '70s. He cranked second ascents of more famous Gill problems than anyone else, such as *Scab* in the Black Hill's Needles and the *Pinch Route* on the Mental Block at Colorado's Horsetooth Reservoir. On the latter he one-upped Gill by starting with both feet on the rock instead of with a swing start.

Williams also hates losing. When he felt others would eclipse his track record he bowed out of bouldering, only to come back 15 years later to feel the joy of burning off kids half his age.

JIM HOLLOWAY—
PURE STRENGTH, PURE MOTIVE

It's one thing to put up problems your peers can't repeat;
quite another to put up problems that have stumped boulderers for 20 years and continue to baffle them. Jim Holloway
took bouldering standards in the '70s and pushed them farther than anyone has before, since, or likely forever. He did
this by competing against himself, not others. He trained
hard, but in primitive fashion, and despite a congenital skeletal defect in his lower spine, reached levels of strength most
'90s climbers only dream of. He could hold a perfect front
lever and a half-minute conversation simultaneously.

Holloway was a purist. He didn't care for ratings, sit-down
starts, cheater stones, or even having a spot. Mention power
spotting and his face registers disgust. He started on the
ground after every attempt. He felt that the honorable way to
establish a new problem was to climb an entirely new stretch
of rock, not just add hard moves to an existing route. He was
known as an exceedingly smooth climber and when told that
he was only so good because he was 6' 4" tall, he would
crunch himself up and send problems using short persons'
sequences. His most stylish trick though, was the way he
would pause in the midst of a crux move, reach back, and
adjust his trademark painter's cap.

BOB MURRAY—
THE FIRST ASCENT MACHINE

Bob Murray is quiet, shy, and a bit of a loner. He prefers to
boulder by himself. He also doesn't care to repeat problems.
He is therefore one of the most prolific boulderers in
American history, having put up hundreds of first ascents.
Compared to Holloway, style didn't carry much weight with
Murray. If a landing looked bad, he was happy to self-belay on
a toprope, and even to hangdog moves while doing so. He
couldn't have cared less what others thought; he just wanted

to climb new problems and do ever thinner and harder moves, preferably dynamics.

Murray looks undernourished until he pulls up on a problem: then muscles seem to come out of nowhere and power him up. His fanatical training begot a remarkable strength-to-weight ratio. Rather than relying entirely on his arms, however, he did many of his desperates barefoot, so he could use his toes like fingers.

In the American Southwest, the term "Murray Problem" is said with reverence. Nonetheless, because Murray never sought publicity and rarely received any, many of his problems may never be found again.

JIM KARN—MOVE MASTER

Jim Karn is best-known for his success as a sport climbing competitor, but he has also compiled one of the best bouldering records of any American in the late '80s and '90s. Karn successfully used an "I'm going to do lame so I've got nothing to lose" attitude to free his mind before sport comps. Winning these competitions was a necessary evil that gained him the financial freedom to pursue other ends, such as bouldering with his friends. Out at the boulders, he ditched the negative energy approach in favor of friendly competition with his bros. They would rip on each other mercilessly, but in good humor, prodding each other to try harder.

Karn rarely uses his strength to put up new problems. To him it doesn't matter who did a move first, only that he himself can do it. He uses boulders as training apparatus, doing multiple laps on hard problems and making those problems even harder by cranking them static or powering past intermediate holds. When he was younger, he sought out ever harder and harder moves to do. Now he looks to master moves and climb as smoothly as possible. To him the best way to do a problem might not be the most efficient way; but rather, the most aesthetic.

JOHN SHERMAN—THE AUTHOR

Perhaps I'm being self-indulgent including myself in this list. If I share two things in common with all of the above climbers, it's that I love bouldering and I have a strong desire to succeed. My style has also been composed of bits and pieces taken from some of those above. Like Murray, I seldom repeat problems, instead preferring to constantly experience new terrain. Like Holloway, I value purity of ascent style. I refuse to use cheater stones or power spots. I have driven many of my spotters nuts if I bump into them: even if my shoelace brushes against them I feel I haven't truly climbed the problem and must try it again "cleanly." One great advantage to such a pure style is that no matter how much flak I caught for my vocal opinions or my brash and unrefined character, I never caught any flak for how I did an ascent.

Unlike most of the above boulderers, I hate to train. At times I have been competitive like Bob Williams (especially when I'm smoking the old geezer off a problem). Then there were all the months spent bouldering alone in the desert during the "Dark Ages" of the mid-'80s, when partners were hard to come by. In those days it was the beauty of the sport alone that drove me on.

Different approaches have worked for me at different times. So far in my career I have visited over 300 bouldering areas and climbed over 10,000 problems, many of them firsts. As it stands now, I wouldn't trade my career for anyone's.

THE BEST ADVICE IN THE BOOK

If you learn only one thing from this book, let it be this: There are many paths to a happy and successful bouldering career—don't try to copy another boulderer's style and technique verbatim. Find what works for you and stick with that. Don't try to become the next Bob Murray or Ben Moon. Forcing yourself to climb like someone you aren't will minimize results. Be yourself instead. Pick the parts of others' styles that work for you; discard those that don't. If your reasons for bouldering change throughout your career, there is nothing wrong with that.

A LAST REMINDER

Bouldering is what you make it each time you go out. Though much of this book is devoted to helping you improve, you needn't be obsessed with always cranking harder and harder problems. There's nothing wrong with spending a session goofing around with your friends, seeing who can run farthest up a slab, or who can climb a problem with a hand in a pocket, and so forth. Above all, bouldering should be fun.

See you out at the boulders…

Appendix

BOULDERING RATINGS

There are several different rating systems at use in America. The two most commonly used are discussed below.

"B" Ratings

John Gill's B system was the first rating system used exclusively on boulder problems. It had three grades: B1, B2, and B3. B1 had moves as hard as the hardest roped climbs of the time. Gill says, "B2 is quite a bit harder. And B3…should be a completely objective climbing rating. B3 is something that is done once, is tried frequently, but is not repeated. If it is repeated, then it drops automatically either to B2 or even B1." (Though Gill's definition of B grades evolved throughout his career, this definition, which appeared in Master of Rock [1977], is the most commonly used.) B grades were intended to slide as standards increased. In 1969 Gill defined B1 as 5.10, in 1977 as 5.11, in 1987 around 5.12. This system allows people to judge themselves against the standards of their own generation. It also points out the fact that a climber doing B2 today is pushing no harder than a climber doing B2 30 years ago, even if today's route is more difficult. The disadvantage with the B system is that it requires constant regrading of problems. The regrading process at most areas (if it occurs at all) does not keep pace with standards; therefore the B2 category gets fatter and fatter. By its very nature, the B system is interpreted differently at different times in the same area.

"V" Ratings

Unlike the sliding scale B system, the V system is open-ended: the bigger the number, the harder the problem. It starts at V0 and currently extends to V14, though someone is sure to claim a bigger number any day. Whether a problem is intimidating, scary, loose, or has a bad landing has no effect on its V rating—only the physical difficulty counts—that is, the technicality of the moves combined with the demands on one's power and endurance. Therefore the rating would remain the same whether the route was toproped or bouldered. Hence, a scary V2 may be more difficult for some to boulder than a safe V5. The V system originated at Hueco Tanks and is currently the most commonly used system in the United States. It has also been adopted in some areas overseas.

WARNING: Boulder problems are hard to rate because dozens of variables can greatly affect how hard an individual finds each single move. As most problems are only a few moves long, a difference in a single move makes a lot more difference than on a full rope-length pitch where such differences tend to even out after many moves. Furthermore, ratings rarely correspond between different areas. Take all ratings with a grain of salt. If you are unsure about a problem's difficulty and your ability to attempt it safely, then pick a different problem you are more comfortable with. View ratings merely as a rough indication of but one component of a problem's overall make-up. Free yourself of preconceived notions of your ability; given time and honest effort, any problem is within reach. Learn to mistrust ratings and pity those who are slaves to them.

If the routes stayed the same, but the gradings were suddenly all switched around, it would be interesting to see which routes people would be trying to do."

—Jim Holloway

SUGGESTED READING

Ament, Pat. *Master of Rock, A Lighthearted Walk Through the Life and Rock Climbing of John Gill.* Adventure's Meaning Press, 1992. The inspirational biography of the ultimate boulderer, John Gill. The extensive photo selection of Gill in action has served as a cult guidebook for boulderers since the original edition of this work appeared in 1977.

Long, John. *How To Rock Climb, Second Edition.* Chockstone Press, 1993. A good primer on movement techniques.

Long, John and Craig Luebben. *Advanced Rock Climbing.* Chockstone Press, 1997. Picks up where How To Rock Climb leaves off.

Sherman, John. *Stone Crusade, A Historical Guide to Bouldering in America.* AAC Press, 1994. A history of American bouldering, complete with directions on how to get to over 50 of America's top bouldering areas. Lots of action photos.